RISJ *CHALL*

Counter-Hegemonic News

A case study of Al-Jazeera English and Telesur

James Painter

Contents:

Figures and Tables

The appendix to this report, containing programme transcripts and summaries, can be found on the Reuters Institute website http://reutersinstitute.politics.ox.ac.uk/counterhegemonicnews.html

Introduction

The content and delivery of news is at present changing more fundamentally than at any time in living memory. The rapid growth in new platforms, such as the internet and mobile phones, the vast increase in the creation and exchange of user-generated content and the steep decline in newspaper consumption in many Western markets are just three of the manifestations of the revolution.

But another change demands attention, and is the focus of this essay. That is the boom in national and particularly international news channels. Much of that boom is commercially funded, especially in South and East Asia. But the year 2006 was also remarkable for the proliferation of new, mainly state-funded TV channels – remarkable not least because it took place during a period of history generally inimical to large-scale investment in public companies.

Some of these channels – I examine two in particular – can be defined as 'counter-hegemonic': that is, they are set up with the explicit intention of challenging the 'BBC/CNN approach' to world events. This challenge can be relatively muted: France 24 was one of the channels to start in 2006, and was seen by both President Jacques Chirac and senior figures in French television as offering a different perspective on world events than that supplied by CNN or the BBC – a need perceived to be the greater because of the sharp division between France and the US/UK on the invasion of Iraq.[1] Sometimes the challenge can be more confrontational: Telesur, as we shall see, is the best example of that. In all cases, however, the assumption is that the 'BBC/CNN model', and its attachment to neutrality, balance and impartiality, is to a greater or lesser extent a sham.

[1] Caroline Wyatt, 'World News to Get a French Flavour', BBC News website (6 Dec. 2006) <http://news.bbc.co.uk/2/hi/europe/6212138.stm>.

Impartiality – the tradition in which I have worked for my professional life – is defined in the BBC's editorial guidelines as lying 'at the heart of the BBC's commitment to its audiences'. The agreement accompanying the BBC Charter requires the BBC

> *to produce comprehensive, authoritative and impartial coverage of news and current affairs in the UK and throughout the world, to support fair and informed debate … the BBC is forbidden from expressing an opinion on current affairs or matters of public policy other than broadcasting.*

In practice, this means supplying 'a properly balanced service consisting of a wide range of subject matter and views broadcast over an appropriate time scale across all our output'; the provision of 'a wide range of opinion … so that no significant strand of thought is knowingly unreflected or under represented' and the avoidance of 'bias or an imbalance of views on controversial subjects'. Importantly,

> *journalists and presenters, including those in news and current affairs, may provide professional judgments but may not express personal opinions on matters of public policy or political or industrial controversy. Our audiences should not be able to tell from BBC programmes or other BBC output the personal views of our journalists and presenters on such matters.*

Of those channels launching, or significantly expanding, in 2006, some more or less follow the BBC/CNN, or 'Western', model of impartiality. These included:
- Germany's public international broadcaster, Deutsche Welle, said it was expanding its Arabic TV operation to 24 hours a day;
- Euronews, which is financed by several European governments, announced its expansion into Spanish and Portuguese to Latin America;
- the BBC World Service, which the British Foreign Office funds, confirmed its diversification from radio into Arabic and Farsi TV.

Those channels which sought, again in different ways, a 'counter-hegemonic' style, included:
- Russia Today, funded by President Putin's government, announced its desire to expand from English into Arabic and Spanish;
- Telesur, bankrolled by President Chávez of Venezuela, expanded its operations across Latin America;

- the Iranian government revealed its intention of starting its own English-language TV channel, which would appear in 2007 as Press TV.

France 24, in which the French government has a large financial stake, falls somewhere between these two models. The main French TV news and current affairs, both on public and private channels, work under a mandate of balance and objectivity: France 24 was not expected to stray far from these aims, but merely – it seemed – give a larger space to official French views. However, its ambitions were later curtailed by President Sarkozy: who said, in January 2008, that broadcasting round the world in English was 'senseless', that the network would be renamed 'France Monde' and would broadcast only in French.[2]

The differences between the second group of channels is more of ideological content than ownership. Most are state-owned – but the first group adheres to principles of impartiality (even if these standards are contested), and spring from a tradition in which broadcasters see their news and current affairs output as a public service, not a state voice. The second group sees the values of impartiality as a cover for Western hegemonic power, and seeks to redress the balance. The members of both groups are all state funded, if in different ways. Fox News, the US 24-hour news and current affairs channel, launched in October 1996, also believes the BBC/CNN claim for impartiality to be a sham – but for very different reasons, seeing both channels as heavily biased towards the liberal-left. It uses the slogan 'fair and balanced' as a sign that it gives a voice to underrepresented opinion on the right. Both Fox and CNN are privately owned.

The arrival of so many channels has raised a number of intriguing questions – including an extensive discussion of whether the proliferation of the new channels is fomenting the emergence of a genuinely global or regional 'public sphere', and if so, of what it consists.[3] There is considerable debate as to whether traditional Western media giants such as CNN, the BBC, Reuters and AP continue to dominate the new media landscape either through their control of picture distribution, or by successful partnerships with local providers where they remain the dominant partner, or by the universalisation of Western news values, or by their large advertising and

[2] 'Sarkozy Says "Non" to France 24', BBC News website (9 Jan. 2008), <http://news.bbc.co.uk/2/hi/europe/7178158.stm>.
[3] Mugdha Rai and Simon Cottle, 'Global Mediations: On the Changing Ecology of Satellite Television News', *Global Media and Communication*, 3/1 (April 2007): pp. 51–78. D. K. Thussu (ed.), *Media on the Move: Global Flow and Contra-Flow* (London and New York: Routledge, 2007). I. Volkmer, 'The Global Network Society and the Global Public Sphere', *Development*, 46/1 (March 2003): pp. 9–16. Colin Sparks, 'Is there a Global Public Sphere?', in D. K. Thussu (ed.), *Electronic Empires: Global Media and Local Resistance* (London: Arnold, 1998), pp. 108–24. James Curran and Myung-Jin Park (eds), *De-Westernising Media Studies* (New York: Routledge, 2000).

3

marketing budgets. A more heterogeneous, hybrid and pluralistic media environment has certainly emerged, as new channels challenge the traditional players in many local or regional markets. But there is much doubt as to whether they generate new contra-flows of information reversing the dominant flow of news from 'the West to the rest'. Most authors are agreed that the flow is more like a trickle restricted to diaspora communities living in the North, but without much impact on host populations.

This study touches on these issues, but three areas particularly are explored which have been less covered. The first of these concerns the editorial content of these new channels. Do they offer a different set of editorial priorities in the selection and treatment of stories? For example, a study of Singapore's Channel News Asia (CNA), which purported to have an Asian vision of the news when it launched in 2000, concluded that CNA was broadly similar to CNN in its presentation and selection of news.[4] Another study of Zee TV, India's first private Hindi-language satellite channel, found that its news bulletins were largely derivative of the style of Western media, adopting similar standards of production and news values.[5] Indeed the same author argues that in many markets the new regionally based channels ape the Western tendency towards 'infotainment' by which the visually appealing, sensationalised news and light treatment of serious issues predominate.[6]

A related, still more important issue is whether these new channels, while offering different news content, follow the same journalistic values espoused by mainstream Western media organisations. Many concerned with developing the new counter-hegemonic news style believe that these values are often flouted by the present dominant networks. The question explored here is how far these new channels, in their broadcasts, seek to remedy that by finding a different style and practice which can fairly be described as impartial – or themselves, deliberately or not, show a bias.

There is a third set of related questions around the aims of these channels, and particularly the ones financed by governments or states. Do those that aim to be counter-hegemonic represent a new age of soft propaganda or 'soft power'? To what extent are they reacting against the domination of a Washington- or London-based international agenda and world view? What does it mean when they say they offer a non-Western perspective to the

[4] The authors concluded that there was no new focus in its treatment of conflicts in Asia, no more positive images of Asia, and no more 'development' news such as education and health issues. They speculated that Asian media organisations had little choice but to present Asia in the way to which audiences were accustomed. K. Natarajan and H. Xiaoming, 'An Asian Voice? A Comparative Study of Channel News Asia and CNN', *Journal of Communication*, 53/2 (2003): pp. 300–14.
[5] D. K. Thussu, 'Localising the Global: Zee TV in India', in Thussu, *Electronic Empires*, pp. 273–94.
[6] D. K. Thussu, 'Live TV and Bloodless Deaths: War, Infotainment and 24/7 News', in D. K. Thussu and D. Freedman (eds), *War and the Media: Reporting Conflict 24/7* (London: Sage, 2003), pp. 117–32.

news? How far does a 'corrective' non-Western version of what constitutes news turn into information that is anti-Western? How do they show, or do they show, that they are independent of their funders? How are they different from state-owned propaganda stations like Cubavisión under Fidel Castro or Radio Moscow under the Communists? In what sense are those that propagate a point of view different from partisan commercial channels like Fox News? There has been considerable research published on several aspects of Al-Jazeera Arabic, but little substantive on the others.[7]

This study is designed to suggest answers to these questions. It is beyond its scope to discuss in depth the key success factors for any channel, or the impact of the new wave of channels in different markets. But it does not start out with an entirely open mind. There is a strong suspicion that many channels are, or will turn out to be, vanity projects with negligible audiences. Many of the new channels hope to emulate AJA's remarkable impact, but few operate in markets which replicate the predominately state-controlled Arab media market which AJA broke open. Second, there seems little doubt that many of the state-funded channels are a means of augmenting national prestige in the way that a national airline might. In some cases, they also exist to propagate a particular political perspective favourable to the funder(s): in that sense, they appear to be an arm of public diplomacy or soft power. However, both of these suppositions need to be tested.

The following chapters focus on two very different examples of the new wave, Telesur and Al-Jazeera English (AJE). Telesur has received little attention outside of Latin America. Based in Caracas, it was launched as a 24/7 channel in October 2005 and funded by the oil money of the '21st century socialist' government of Venezuela's President Hugo Chávez. It is the first of its kind to emerge from Latin America. It says it is offering a different vision of news from CNN or the BBC, without violating internationally accepted journalistic principles such as accuracy and balance. Telesur provides an interesting case study as it fits the pattern seen in other parts of the world of state-funded TV stations providing an additional voice and perspective. This perspective is not presented in the dull, dirigiste style of communist propaganda of old. Indeed, the channel adopts many of the trappings of the more established channels.

---

[7] Amongst the most recent are Naomi Sakr, 'Al-Jazeera: Challenger or Lackey?', in D. K. Thussu, *Media on the Move*, pp 116–32. Marc Lynch, *Voices of the New Arab Public* (New York: Columbia University Press, 2006). Hugh Miles, *Al-Jazeera: How Arab TV News Challenged the World* (London: Abacus, 2005) and Mohamed Zayani (ed.), *The Al-Jazeera Phenomenon: Critical Perspectives on New Arab Media* (London: Pluto, 2005).

Ever since the debate kicked off in the 1980s over a New World Information and Communication Order (NWICO), there has been plenty of discussion around the existence or desirability of a 'non-Western' or 'Southern' perspective on news. For the first time since the beginning of that debate, a well-funded channel exists, Al-Jazeera English, which promises to mark a radical change by offering a version of this 'non-Western' or 'Southern' take on the news. Unlike Telesur, AJE operates in the global Anglophone market and enjoys considerably more editorial freedom from its paymaster. But like Telesur, it is aiming to offer something different to the BBC and CNN, albeit without a strongly partisan perspective. Its distinctiveness lies more in this new editorial perspective than any other aspect of the channel. The precise nature of its editorial vision is hard to pin down at times, but AJE is arguably by far the most interesting development of the last few decades in the attempt to provide news 'from the south'.

Chapter 1 of this study places the arrival of AJE and Telesur into the context of the general boom in international news channels. Chapter 2 gives an overview of the first year of AJE's operations with a particular emphasis on its distinctive editorial perspective, and Chapter 3 provides the content analysis of some of its news programmes, from different months of 2007. Chapter 4 outlines the more specific political and media context into which Telesur was born, while Chapter 5 analyses the editorial content of some of its news programmes broadcast in October and November 2006. Finally, I draw out some of the conclusions about both Telesur and AJE and their wider significance. It should be stressed that, as many media analysts have experienced, doing detailed content analysis of broadcast programmes can be more demanding, particularly of time, than with the printed word. As will be seen from Chapters 3 and 5, the samples taken may not be large enough to give definitive answers to some of the editorial questions posed, but they are certainly sufficient to suggest some trends.

The importance of these developments for journalism is large, for two reasons. First, there is a growing view that 'opinionated news' is becoming more popular than fair, balanced and neutral news, especially among the young. Fox News is now the market leader in cable news in the US, prompting the longer established CNN to have more opinionated anchors on their shows; and in its June 2007 report, '*New News, Future News*', the UK communications regulator Ofcom suggested that impartiality may now be seen by young people, and ethnic minorities, as repellent, and contribute to disengagement.

It argued that

> *impartiality, if applied across the board, may come to be seen as a possible hindrance to a truly diverse news supply and will, in any case, be increasingly difficult to enforce ... it is also possible that universal application of impartiality rules may become less appropriate in the future, as more and more sources of audiovisual news content – some regulated for impartiality and others not – are accessed side-by-side.*[8]

This tendency – so far sternly resisted by most European public service broadcasters – is likely to become more pronounced: we should understand where it comes from, and how the opinionated channels work.

Second, the principle of balance, fairness and neutrality is always a contested one. To broadcast news is to choose, and to choose severely, among a host of possible events, ways of framing them and duration of time spent revealing and explaining them. In explaining the difference France 24 would make, one of its presenters, the former UK television journalist Mark Owen, said:

> *Take the conflict in Lebanon this summer. If Jacques Chirac's call for a ceasefire – which didn't even make BBC or CNN – had been reported earlier, it could have brought about an earlier resolution of the conflict. If Chirac's call had been reported more widely it maybe could have saved thousands of lives. That was a story calling out for a French angle, given the historic links to Lebanon.*[9]

Those who cleave to the ideal that impartiality can be preserved must understand the critique from those broadcasters, journalists and politicians who do not. Thus how these channels work and our conclusions on how far they have managed to 'break the mould' are crucial to the future of journalism – everywhere.

---

[8] Ofcom, *New News, Future News: The Challenges for Television News after Digital Switch-Over*, London: Ofcom (26 June 2007), pp. 5.

[9] Angelique Chrisafis, 'The News through French Eyes: Chirac TV Takes on "Anglo-Saxon Imperialism"', *Guardian* (6 Dec. 2006).

[10] Rai and Cottle, 'Global Mediations'. There has been much press speculation about the arrival of an African 24/7 channel, known as A24, in 2008, largely through the efforts of Salim Amin. See Chris Cramer, 'Africa on a Roll', *Guardian* (24 Sept. 2007). The South African Broadcasting Corporation (SABC) also plans to launch a 24-hour news and current affairs TV channel sometime in 2008.
[11] There are three others owned by private capital (Globovisión in Caracas, Todo Noticias in Buenos Aires and Globonews in Brazil). They do have some reach outside their country base, but this is mostly restricted to diaspora communities.

1 The Boom in 24/7s

Since CNN started in 1980 as the first global TV news channel (BBC World was launched, as BBC World Service TV, in 1991), the number of regional or international channels which are predominately news stations has grown to more than 100 (see Figure 1.1). Much of the boom is recent, and has taken place in South and East Asia. Most noticeably there are now more than thirty, virtually all commercial, stations in India, and six in Taiwan alone. While Asia and Europe are well-populated, Oceania has only a handful and Africa none.[10] In Latin America there is only Telesur as a pan-regional channel.[11]

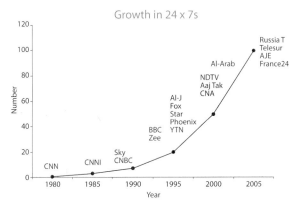

Figure 1.1. The growth in 24/7 news channels, 1980–2006 (adapted from Chart 1 in Rai and Cottle, 'Global Mediations'). The numbers of channels are approximate.

It is an obvious but often overlooked point that there is a huge variation in the types of channels born out of the boom. Some clearly have to a lesser or greater degree a political agenda, but they are also very different in terms of reach (global, regional or local), finance base (state, private or mixed), type of ownership, range of languages, market profile, target audience, content (type of news genre, programme offer, production values, format, presentation style, localised versus international), multimedia offer (including methods of engaging with the audience), news-gathering capacity, international affiliation, technological framework, and crucially, standards of journalism. For established international channels entering regional markets, the different types of 'localisation' are also important (local advertising, local dubbing or subtitling, local programming and opt-outs).[12]

The reasons for the growth in these channels are also diverse. But there are some features common to different markets to do with aspects of globalisation, the falling costs of communication satellites, the spread of digital technology, and the deregulation of many broadcasting and telecommunications sectors. The desire for influence and prestige on the part of some governments which have become cash-rich due to the high price of oil and gas (Venezuela, Qatar, Iran and Russia) is hugely important in the case of Telesur, Al-Jazeera, Press TV and Russia Today. The steady increase in the number of households with satellite or cable television is another factor, as are the changing viewing patterns which require news on demand.[13]

Then there is the significance of worldwide migration which, according to the UN, reached 200 million people in 2005. Among these, the higher income groups can form a natural market for some channels. Indeed, the Phoenix news channel in Mandarin and Zee TV in Hindi specifically target the diaspora Mandarin- and Hindi-speaking communities (there are thought to be 35 million Indians and 25 million Chinese living outside their home countries).[14] In September 2007, NDTV, India's largest private news channel, announced a new satellite channel, mostly in English, targeting the millions of South Asian expatriates living in the Middle East and Africa.

The growth in news channels in Europe largely took place in the 1990s as result of commercial, technological and regulatory changes. Very few have a regional presence (Euronews is an exception), partly for linguistic reasons. The Indian market in contrast has a remarkably broad range of

---

[12] Jean Chalaby, 'Transnational Television in Europe: The Role of Pan-European Channels', *European Journal of Communication,* 17/2 (2002): pp. 183–203.
[13] It should not of course be forgotten that in many parts of the developing world watching TV via cable or satellite remains an elite activity. Less than 1% of TV households in sub-Saharan Africa subscribed to pay-TV services in 2007, compared to 15% in Eastern Europe, 20% in Latin America, 36% in Western Europe and 93% in the USA.
[14] Thussu, *Media on the Move,* ch. 1.

	AJA	AJE	BBCW	CCTV-9	CNNI	Euronews	France24	Press TV	Russia T	Telesur
Nature of Funding	State	State	Mixed	State	Commercial	Mixed	Mixed	State	State	State
Main operations base	Doha	Doha	London	Beijing	Atlanta	Lyon	Paris	Tehran	Moscow	Caracas
Main language	Arabic	English	English	English	English	Various	English	English	English	Spanish
Annual Budget (US$)	120m	n.a.	130m	n.a.	>200m[a]	75m	127m	n.a.	40m	10m (e)
Overseas bureaux	65[b]	65[b]	72	18[c]	30[d]	0	0	12	6	11
Reporters worldwide	600[b]	600[b]	650[e]	50 (e)	170[d]	0	150[f]	26	n.a.	>20
Main target countries	M. East	World	World	World	World	Europe	World	World	Europe/US	Lat. Am.
Weekly audience	>40m	n.a.[g]	78m	n.a.	>100m	7m[g]	n.a.[g]	n.a.	n.a.	<1m (e)
Reach (households)	>100m	113m	161m	60m	200m	200m	80m	n.a.	90m	2–3m

Notes: Figures are official unless otherwise stated; (e) = estimate.

a   CNNI's total programming costs in 2002 were US$220m.
b   Combined totals for AJA and AJE.
c   Figure for overseas bureaux for whole CCTV network.
d   Overseas staff correspondents, not US bureaux.

e   Includes BBC World Service overseas reporters.
f   France 24 can call on correspondents from Radio France Internationale, Agence France-Press and others.
g   European Media and Marketing Survey in 2007 gave AJE and France 24 an audience of c.1m each.

Table 1.1: Ten main international news channels compared

channels, segmented by language, geography and genre (current affairs or business news). A market survey commissioned by the BBC World Service in 2006 estimated there were 31 players across various languages offering mostly India-centric news.[15] More recent studies put the number higher.[16] The boom has largely been driven by private investors taking advantage of deregulation in the Indian media market. But there are other factors such as the rapid increase in the number of middle-income Indians and the number of households with cable TV,[17] the high advertising revenue per viewer in the news genre, falling start-up costs, and in some cases, the financial support of local politicians. For most of 2006, two Indian stations were the market leaders (Aaj Tak in Hindi and NDTV in English). CNN International and BBC World[18] had been relegated to being minor players, although CNN's local partnership with IBN had given it a strong market presence (in second place to NDTV in 2006).

The boom in Asia is largely commercially driven. But there are two important exceptions: the state-financed channels in India and China, fore-runners of a trend in the 'BRICs' – Brazil, Russia, India and China, all strongly developing economies. All of these have either started, or are talking about starting, their own international channels. The oldest of these is the Chinese CCTV-9 which began broadcasting in English in 2000, but was revamped in 2004 as part of a shift from the defensive to the offensive in its foreign policy.[19] Its aims are to give a Chinese perspective on world affairs and to break the Western voice's monopoly on the news (i.e. those of CNN and the BBC). It certainly does not report anything anti-government or anti-party.[20] A typical example of its output could be found on 4 May 2007, when it reported the findings of the IPCC climate change report in a similar style to BBC World and other international channels, but focused heavily on the view of a Chinese government official.[21]

---

[15] Eleven were national stations in Hindi (nine current affairs, two business news), six were national stations in English (four current affairs, two business news), while fourteen were regional.
[16] See for example, D. K. Thussu, *News as Entertainment: The Rise of Global Infotainment*, London: Sage, 2007, ch. 4, 'Indian Infotainment'. Thussu points out that much of the news content of such channels consists of the three 'C's: cricket, cinema and crime.
[17] In 2006, there were an estimated 60 million subscribers in India, the third largest market in the world.
[18] BBC World was renamed BBC World News in April 2008.
[19] Xiaoling Zhang, 'CCTV International and Public Diplomacy', paper given at SOAS conference, 'International Broadcasting, Public Diplomacy and Cultural Exchange', London (19 Dec. 2007).
[20] Former controller Jiang Heping, as quoted in the Vivien Cui, 'CCTV Tries to Shed its Mouthpiece Image', *South China Morning Post* (6 April 2004).
[21] There was no criticism of China's actions at the IPCC meetings or of its policies towards the environment. Several international channels included mention of China's alleged obstructionist role in the negotiations over the final wording of the impact report, but CCTV had no mention of this. See James Painter, 'All Doom and Gloom? International TV coverage of the April and May 2007 IPCC reports', paper presented at the Environmental Change Institute's Conference, 'Carbonundrums: Making Sense of Climate Change Reporting around the World', Oxford (27 June 2007).

In several markets state-funded channels have staged a remarkable resurgence, given that many analysts had predicted their slow decline or increasing irrelevance. A large part of the reason for this is that high levels of gas or oil revenues are in effect funding Russia Today, Al-Jazeera and Telesur. President Chávez is reported to have spent over US$20bn in overseas projects,[22] President Putin enjoyed a current account surplus of more than US$80bn at the end of 2005, while Qatar's was US$12.5bn. A budget of US$30–50m, or even US$100m, a year to run an international news channel represents a small fraction of these surpluses, and considerably less than the expense of running a diplomatic service.

Russia Today launched its English operation in December 2005. Its start-up and annual running costs of around US$30-40m were nominally provided 50 per cent by state money and 50 per cent by commercial banks, but in reality the Kremlin funded it. It was part of a process by which banks and companies friendly to the government were encouraged to invest in 'national projects'. Several Western journalists were employed alongside Russian colleagues with the main aim of giving the news, particularly to foreign visitors, from a Russian perspective and in a style more palatable to an international audience.

No independent studies have been made of its content or reach, but those who have worked there or watched the station say its coverage of international affairs, and particularly of Iran, Iraq and the rest of the Middle East, gives a Russian slant to the news.[23] It is clearly designed to promote Putin's and Russia's view of the world, and in this sense is an instrument of foreign policy. Coverage of Russian news includes little criticism of Putin or Russia's actions in Chechnya, and so mirrors most domestic TV coverage which avoids thorough analysis of 'difficult' subjects such as racial tension or media freedom.

Like Russia Today, France 24 (launched in December 2006 with a reported US$100m annual budget) was also seen as offering a different perspective to the news to be distinguished from the 'Anglo-Saxon channels, such as CNN, the BBC, Fox News or to the one of Al-Jazeera'.[24] Unlike Russia Today, its financing was partly private as ownership is to be shared 50/50 by the commercial network TF1 and the state-funded company France Télévisions. Its genesis was in part due to President Chirac's anger at the

---

[22] The figure is taken from the Caracas-based Center for Economic Investigations, quoted in Juan Forero, 'Chávez Using Oil Money to Buy Influence Abroad', *International Herald Tribune* (5 April 2006).
[23] Russia has closer relationships with Hamas, Iran and Syria than Washington would like. Roula Khalaf and Arkady Ostrovsky, 'Russia Targets Middle East with Arabic TV Channel', *Financial Times* (15 June 2006).
[24] Leigh Holmwood, 'Chirac Takes on CNN', *Guardian* (16 Oct. 2006).

way the French government's policy was misrepresented or under-reported in the run-up to the second Gulf war. According to one observer, the channel was part of Chirac's legacy of 'projects that continue France's struggle against the global domination of the US'.[25]

Journalists at France 24 were reported to have to sign the station's charter pledging to give a specifically French view of the news based on the 'fundamental values of France', but this apparently does not entail government interference in editorial matters.[26] Cynics noted that, for a station promoting all things French, it was odd that its second channel was broadcasting 75 per cent in English. An Arabic channel was launched in April 2007, with Spanish to follow in 2009, with the clear intention of having influence in various markets. However, all these plans were brought into question in January 2008 when President Sarkozy announced he was in favour of closing France 24 and pooling its resources with France's other international broadcasters RFI and TV5 under a new brand 'France Monde', which would speak only French.[27]

No detailed study of its output has been published but some impressionistic accounts detected no excessive reporting of the views of the French government or politicians, or indeed excessive coverage of French foreign policy or domestic issues. French 'values' were mostly to be seen in programmes on French lifestyle and culture. One observer saw no evidence of it being either anti-American or overwhelmingly pro-Arab. Rather, he felt it was 'bland and anonymous, with a low-cost, voice-over feel'.[28] The result, he said, was 'low-impact television'.

France 24 saw itself as similar to Telesur, CCTV-9 and Russia Today in being 'counter-hegemonic', in the sense of offering a different vision or news content to the main Western media like CNN and the BBC. But unlike the other three, France 24 seemed to be loyal to journalistic values of plurality of opinion and impartiality. As will be discussed later, AJE also clearly aims to be counter-hegemonic in the sense of competing with CNN and the BBC, although it was not a priority for Al-Jazeera Arabic when it was launched in 1996.[29] AJA's early emphasis was on pluralistic reporting and (purported) editorial independence from its Sandhurst-educated benefactor, Sheikh Hamad bin Khalifa al Thani, the emir of Qatar.

---

[25] Chrisafis, 'News through French Eyes'.

[26] 'International TV News Channel Set to be on Air by End of 2006', *Le Monde* website (15 Sept. 2006), <http://mondediplo.com/>.

[27] At the time of writing, it was not clear what model of public channel Sarkozy would choose.

[28] John Vincour, 'A French View of the News that is Pretty Much Like the Old Ones', *International Herald Tribune* (2 Jan. 2007). The channel is often seen as suffering from a small budget for overseas reporting. For a more positive appraisal, see James Robinson, 'A French World View, Around the Clock', *Observer* (22 April 2007).

[29] Sakr, 'Challenger or Lackey?', pp. 129.

AJA's rise to prominence has been well-documented. It has a measured audience of 40–50 million viewers mostly in the Arab world. One advertising industry website has said it is the world's fifth most recognised brand. There is no doubt it has completely revolutionised the Arab TV market and opened up a media public sphere in the sense used by Jürgen Habermas, by creating an unprecedented space for pan-Arabic public discussion.[30] Its success is also one of the reasons behind the huge boom in satellite channels in the Arab world. In 2006 there were estimated to be more than 260 satellite channels available on Nilesat and Arabsat, of which about 20 are all-news.

The interesting point to note is that the most important of the news channels receive significant funding from governments or businessmen close to governments: Al-Arabiya (Al-Jazeera's most serious rival backed by a group of Arab businessmen including Sheikh Walid al-Ibrahim, a brother-in-law of King Fahd of Saudi Arabia), Al-Alam (financed by the Iranian government), Al-Manar (a pro-Hezbollah station based in Beirut but financed indirectly by Iran), and Al-Ekhbariya (financed by the Saudi government). Al-Jazeera and Al-Arabiya receive an undisclosed but important revenue flow from advertising but it is doubtful any of the above would survive as commercial operations without state or quasi-state funding.

The Arab media market is clearly a contested space for different local and international governments waging a 'soft' war, parallel to the real conflicts being played out in the region.[31] It is of huge significance that many Western governments are expanding their international broadcasting operations in pursuit of 'soft power' in the Middle East. Most notable is al-Hurra, the US-funded station which has made little impact amongst audiences. As already mentioned, the BBC World Service, Russia Today, France 24 and Deutsche Welle have, or are intending to, expand, their presence in Arabic in the region. The changing geopolitical priorities of Western governments are clearly driving part of the boom.

The launch in July 2007 of the Iranian Press TV, a 24-hour English-language channel funded by President Ahmadinejad, is largely a political response by a government under siege from the Bush administration. But it also sees itself as countering the 'global media stranglehold of Western outlets', including Al-Jazeera English.[32] Like Telesur funded by Ahmadinejad's close ally Hugo Chávez, Press TV is also counter-hegemonic in the sense of being anti-US. Ahmadinejad went further in advocating a political agenda for the channel, when he said it 'should stay beside the oppressed people of the world'.

[30] Ibid., and Lynch, *Voices of the New Arab Public.*
[31] For a useful overview, see Annabelle Sreberny, 'War by Other Means', *The Times Higher* (12 Oct. 2007).
[32] Nazila Fathi, 'Iran Expands Role in Media, via Satellite and in English', *New York Times* (3 July 2007).

A much under-researched area of investigation is whether the state-funded channels have any real impact in their markets. Are the public really interested in watching such channels? Most aspire, of course, to replicate AJA's success. One can argue about the relative weight of the different factors behind its success but they include the following: large-scale funding was a necessary but not sufficient condition, as was an enhanced news-gathering capacity in such trouble spots as Iraq, Afghanistan and the Occupied Territories at crucial moments. A common language spoken across a large number of countries also helped. High production values from news staff trained at the BBC was also significant.

But there is almost universal agreement amongst analysts that the overriding factor behind AJA's success was the state of the Arab media market before it arrived. With some minor exceptions, there was little space for criticism of governments or public debate. Much of AJA's popularity stems from its talk shows where 'opinion and counter-opinions' are freely debated in a loud, plebiscitary manner. It broke the mould and offered a voice to a large sector of the population which did not have one. In many ways it plugged into, but did not create, the anger many viewers felt at the political situation they found in the region. Its frequent irreverence towards many Arab governments was a radical departure from the pattern of state-controlled and policed television. It did not matter too much that its funder, the Qatari government, was seldom scrutinised, as Qatar rarely generated news of regional, let alone international, importance. It is very hard to see where this particular combination of circumstances is repeated in other parts of the world. It is also difficult to see how most, if not all, of the channels funded by states or governments would survive commercially without such heavy financial support.

2 Al-Jazeera English

I tell people that Al-Jazeera provides a different perspective to CNN but an equally valid one. CNN films the launch of the missile. Al-Jazeera films what happens when it lands. (Josh Rushing, Al-Jazeera's US defence and military correspondent, quoted in the Financial Times, 4 Aug. 2007)

The same but different?

If the quantity of media coverage around the launch of a new product could on its own guarantee market success, then Al-Jazeera English (AJE)'s future seemed rosy indeed. But in all the hype over its long-delayed launch on 15 November 2006, the exact nature of AJE's editorial perspective tended to get overlooked in favour of other, more headline-grabbing concerns. Unsurprisingly, the channel's financial capacity to sign big name presenters such as David Frost, Rageh Omaar, Riz Khan and David Marash attracted a lion's share of the coverage. Rumours of tension between AJE's predominately Anglo-Saxon management and executives from its Arab founding partner over control over AJE's direction also proved an attractive angle to report.[33] In the United States, particular attention was paid to how AJE could secure viewers in the US market, given Al-Jazeera Arabic (AJA)'s reputation there as a mouthpiece for terrorists and a purveyor of anti-US propaganda.[34]

However, in a series of interviews given by senior AJE executives around the time of the launch, a clear message was propagated that AJE would offer a 'different perspective' on the news. Although individual

[33] See for example, Owen Gibson and Afshin Rattansi, 'Look East', *Media Guardian* (13 Nov. 2006).
[34] See for example, Howard Kurtz, 'Al-Jazeera Finds its English Voice', *Washington Post* (8 Oct. 2006).

executives stressed diverse aspects of what this 'different perspective' would consist of, in summary it could be described as:

(1) covering the same international events or news in an alternative way to the 'Western perspective' of CNN and BBC World (BBCW);

(2) covering parts of the world which tend not to get reported;

(3) covering developing countries in an original way.

The first aspect was underpinned by the deployment of multicultural staff in four production centres in Kuala Lumpur, Doha, London and Washington, which would not only alternate as the lead presenter of the news at different times of the 24-hour cycle, but would also, in theory at least, offer a different perspective on the top news stories of the moment. Sceptics pointed out that basing two of the four centres in the West ran the risk of restricting any fresh perspective on world news. But as AJE's first managing director Nigel Parsons expressed it, the overall aim was to enable 'viewers to put on different spectacles'.[35] In addition, the hope was that the channel would be able to present on screen, for example, Africans reporting on Africa and Asians reporting on Asia, and thereby counter the predominance of Anglo-Saxon reporters employed around the world by the BBC and CNN.

To bolster the second aim, AJE would put more news-gathering capacity into countries or regions like Darfur, Myanmar (Burma) and Zimbabwe which, either through neglect, practical difficulties of access or an outright ban, other international channels tended not to cover in a detailed or sustained way. AJE was clearly at a considerable advantage to many Western-based news organisations which in recent years have been busy cutting their budgets for overseas reporting. Its considerable financial resources gave AJE the potential at least of being able to drive its own news agenda by having more of its own bureaux in developing countries and thereby not having to rely on pictures from the two main providers, APTN and Reuters.[36] This would allow it in theory to devote considerably more air time than its rivals to news from developing countries in Asia, Africa and Latin America, compared to events in the USA, Europe and other industrialised countries.

The third aspect could probably be best summed up by the familiar phrase long-championed by many African journalists that 'there is more to Africa than AIDs, famine and war'. This would not necessarily mean 'good news stories' from developing countries, but rather a fresher perspective offering new angles and more diversity. Although not a news programme,

---

[35] Quoted in John Kampfner, 'Al-Jazeera's New Voice', *New Statesman* (13 Nov. 2006).

[36] AJE executives do not publicly discuss their budgets, but press reports suggest the total start-up costs were between US$500 million and $1,000 million. By early 2008, they said they had more than 60 overseas bureaux, some of which were shared with AJA.

Witness presented by Rageh Omaar captured some of the essence of this approach: 'human stories made by storytellers from all walks of life', uncluttered by academics or commentators.[37]

Much of the initial monitoring of AJE in the Western press found little fault with its editorial balance. A commentator in *The Times* called the first day 'slick, but depressing', but had no quarrel politically with its coverage of the Middle East, or with the language used.[38] Lawrence Pintak, director of the Kamal Adham Center for Journalism Training and Research at the American University in Cairo, wrote in *Der Spiegel* that there was no evidence of 'anti-American or anti-Israel bias on the new channel'.[39] But Pintak added that AJE's weakness lay not in bias, but in the breadth and depth of news coverage. He complained that major stories from the United States and Western Europe were not covered, and concluded that the channel was in danger of trading a Western-centric view for one preoccupied with the Middle East and Africa.

After a week of watching, Pintak described AJE as looking like 'Bob Geldof TV' as it was 'heavy on compassion but light on news', 'beginning to resemble a UN video service', and accused it of pursuing a 'self-conscious – sometimes excruciating – emphasis on being the un-CNN'.[40] Mark Lawson in the *Guardian* expressed similar concerns about news priorities when he described the first day's reporting as 'unbalanced in its concentration on [the Middle East] and the resulting almost contemptuous attitude to US and UK affairs'.[41] He added that such an approach could limit its audience. The question, he wrote, is 'whether enough Anglophone viewers resent the Anglophone bias of conventional news sufficiently to want this alternative'.

A more detailed assessment after one month's broadcasting was provided by BBC Monitoring on 14 December 2006.[42] The main observations were that:

- AJE had 'kept its pledge to be the voice of the south'. Although the Middle East figured prominently, every news bulletin appeared to make an attempt to have at least one story from Asia and from Latin America. News from Africa was not quite so frequent.
- There was relatively little reporting of mainstream political developments in Europe and the USA.

[37] Brian Whitaker, 'Same News, Different Perspectives', *Guardian* (6 Feb. 2006).
[38] Michael Binyon, '"Slick But Depressing": A First View of English al-Jazeera', *The Times* (15 Nov. 2006).
[39] Lawrence Pintak, 'A CNN for the Developing World', <www.spiegel.de/international>, 16 Nov. 2006.
[40] Lawrence Pintak, "Will Al-Jazeera English Find its Groove?", *Columbia Journalism Review* (30 Nov. 2006).
[41] Mark Lawson, 'Al-Jazeera Launch', *Guardian* (16 Nov. 2006).
[42] Steve Metcalf, 'Al-Jazeera English and Arabic New Coverage Compared', *BBC Monitoring* (14 Dec. 2006).

- In comparison with its sister station, AJA, AJE's coverage of the Middle East was not as extensive or in depth, and it was slightly more restrained in its choice of both language and pictures.
- The presentation was professional and sedate. A typical 30-minute bulletin would have four or five main stories taking up five minutes each. Not all the reports were straight news pieces; many consisted of in-depth current affairs features with no particular news peg.

On its first anniversary, a batch of articles in the media gave AJE managers another good promotional opportunity to emphasize again what they regarded as the editorial essence of the channel after twelve months of bedding down.[43] They stressed traditional highly valued news performance indicators such as scoops (for example, undercover reporters in Myanmar, in Gaza to cover Hamas' takeover, and in Afghanistan with the Taliban) and special in-depth reporting (Somalia and the Pakistan army's raid on the Red Mosque). As a badge of honour, celebrity news (Paris Hilton or OJ Simpson) had been deliberately eschewed. But they also made a conscious effort to provide more ballast to the nature of AJE's editorial distinctiveness:

- AJE's 'different' perspective on the news;
- their rivals' focus on the USA, Western Europe and other industrialised powers, in comparison to the higher percentage of stories AJE covers from outside those areas;
- AJE's coverage of stories the world rarely looks at (to which AJE returns);
- AJE's greater depth of coverage of fewer stories;
- AJE's desire to give more 'voice to the voiceless'.

Again, few of AJE's critics complained that its coverage, including that of the Middle East, was not balanced, or that at least it did not aim to be so.[44] A considerable feather in its cap was an op-ed piece in the *New York Times* arguing that AJE should be widely available in the US, in part because 'America … needs to watch Al Jazeera to understand how the world has changed'.[45] The author, Roger Cohen, argued that 'over all, its striving for balanced reporting from a distinct perspective seems genuine'. Further-more, some observers noted that AJE had a softer line than AJA in its Sunni versus Shia reportage (in which AJA is often accused of following a slight

[43] Articles included 'Al-Jazeera English Turns One, Looks to "strong foothold" in US', *Gulf Times* (16 Nov. 2007); 'Al Jazeera English: The First Year', *Arab Media and Society* (Oct. 2007); James Robinson, 'The Only Country we haven't been Kicked out of is Israel', *Observer* (4 Nov. 2007); interview with David Marash, *Nightline*, National Public Radio (NPR) (14 Nov. 2007). AJE's first anniversary video on its web-site stressed three aspects: setting the news agenda, a fresh perspective and shedding light on under-reported parts of the world.
[44] The few exceptions were some right-wing commentators in the USA. See for example Louis Wittig, who detected a 'distinctly pro-Arab bias', as quoted in Aaron Barnhart, 'Al-Jazeera English: Why One Channel Can Make a World of Difference', *Kansas City Star* (1 July 2007).
[45] Roger Cohen, 'Bring the Real World Home', *New York Times* (12 Nov. 2007).

pro-Sunni, anti-Shiite bias).[46] Its coverage of Iran was seen as offering more context to understanding President Ahmadinejad's policies on nuclear energy and other issues, without crossing the line into general sympathy for him by not broadcasting criticism of his regime.[47]

AJE reporters in the West Bank did occasionally lapse into using the emotive word 'martyr' to describe the Palestinians dying in the fight against Israelis, but this seems to have been an exception.[48] One study of AJE's online site compared to those of the BBC and CNN concluded that AJE refrained from using such non-neutral terms, and in general 'departs from its reporting in Arabic where vocabulary with emotive and historical context is employed widely'.[49] Another study carried out by Arab Media Watch in 2007 of AJE's website concluded that it was 'almost even in the amount of space it gave both viewpoints (52% for Palestinians, 48% for Israelis)'.[50]

Some of the criticisms of AJE focused less on its journalistic values, and more on its *lack* of sufficient distinctiveness from CNN International (CNNI) and BBC World.[51] The format and tone of its news programme were clearly not dissimilar to those of its rivals (albeit presented in High Definition). Moreover, the style of reporting by its correspondents did not seem to be breaking new ground.[52] A high percentage of its main presenters and reporters seemed to be Western in ethnic background, although AJE management went out of their way to stress the variety of nationalities represented amongst their staff. Officially, this is 45 ethnic groups in a staff of more than 1,000, although this disguises the relative importance of each group in senior positions in management, presentation or foreign reporting. There are undoubtedly more correspondents and reporters recruited from

---

[46] See for example Dina Matar, quoted in Paul Gibbs, 'Jazz Band Struggles for Rhythm', *Guardian* (19 Feb. 2007).

[47] AJE producers interviewed by the author said that at editorial meetings they were never instructed to follow a particular editorial line on Iran's President Ahmadinejad or any other government.

[48] See for example the discussion programme on NPR, Talk of the Nation, 'Al-Jazeera English Struggles for U.S. Airtime', broadcast on 4 June 2008.

[49] Leon Barkho, 'Unpacking the Discursive and Social Links in BBC, CNN and Al-Jazeera's Middle East Reporting', *Journal of Arab and Muslim Media Research*, 1/1 (Dec. 2007): pp. 11–30. However, some observers question the validity of drawing too definitive conclusions from the comparison of websites as the stories are very reliant on agency copy and not original material.

[50] Arab Media Watch, 'Palestinian and Israeli Viewpoints in the Media' (Oct. 2007), available at <http://www.arabmediawatch.com/amw/Portals/0/documents/media/20070913SourcesStudyReport.pdf>

[51] See for example, Gibbs, 'Jazz Band Struggles for Rhythm'.

[52] The reporting style of AJE correspondents seems to be more akin to the 'realist' style of BBC reporters where the reporter tends to be omniscient, rather than the 'naturalist' style where the report provides a representation of the world as it might be directly experienced. For a discussion of the difference as seen in BBC and Swedish TV news reports in 2004, see Alexa Robertson, 'Reporting the World Back to Itself', paper presented at SOAS conference, London, (17 Dec. 2007). Nor does AJE's reporting seem to fit the category of 'peace journalism' as espoused by authors like Jake Lynch.

their home regions than appear on BBCW or CNNI.[53] But both AJE's first and second managing director are Western (Nigel Parsons and Tony Burman), its main presenters are Western, the main output editors are Western, there were several examples of Western presenters or special correspondents being flown in to present from developing countries in turmoil, and there seemed to be few, if any, AJE correspondents from the 'south' based in the 'north' giving a 'southern perspective' on the 'north'.

Moreover, AJE did not seem to be experimenting with new forms of interactivity or audience participation in its programmes or programming. Its website is not regarded as particularly innovative in its design, content or interactivity. AJE executives have said privately that the priority in the first year of operations lay in getting its TV journalism right.

In summary, there are strong arguments for suggesting that AJE's distinctiveness from its Western rivals lies more in its editorial perspective than in its programme formats, reporting style or staff profile. Certainly its official slogan 'Setting the news agenda' would suggest that it wants to be perceived this way. The slogan stands out in sharp contrast to BBC World's 'Putting news first' and CNN's 'The most trusted name in news'. It implies that it is in part trying to offer a new version of what is news.

The voice of the south?

Part of AJE's editorial identity clearly consisted of its 'otherness' to the news content or perspective followed by the main Western media like the BBC and CNN. In that limited sense, part of AJE's *raison d'être* was not that dissimilar to the 'counter-hegemonic' vision of other state-financed channels like Telesur, France 24, Russia Today or Press TV. At times too, some of the discourse was reminiscent of the second sense of 'counter-hegemonic', namely the reversal of the dominant information flows from the 'West to the rest'. Sue Phillips, AJE's London bureau chief, told the *Guardian* that the goal was to bring 'the south to the north, rather than the other way round'.[54] There was no hint of Phillips or anyone else of senior standing in AJE using neo-Marxist concepts of information imperialism,[55] but the idea of reversing the normal patterns of news coverage was clearly a key part of AJE's mission. However, nowhere was AJE's editorial perspective described as 'counter-hegemonic' in the narrow sense of being anti-America as the

---

[53] For example, in the programmes monitored in the next chapter, AJE's Kamil Hyder in Pakistan stands out in contrast to the white, male Western correspondents from the BBC (Chris Morris) and CNN (Karl Penhaul).

[54] Gibson and Rattansi, 'Look East'.

[55] For an understanding of the concept, see for example Oliver Boyd-Barrell, 'Media Imperialism Reformulated', in D. K. Thussu (ed.), *Electronic Empires*, pp. 157–76.

dominant world power. In this way, AJE's editorial purpose was clearly different to that of Telesur's.

AJE was at pains to show that its otherness did not lie in being a propaganda channel, and that it followed the same rules on accuracy, impartiality and plurality espoused by traditional Western-based media. Its code of ethics published on its website speaks of adhering to the 'journalistic values of honesty, courage, fairness, balance, independence, credibility and diversity', and of presenting 'diverse points of view and opinions without bias or partiality'.[56] Such a heady combination of editorial distinctiveness and traditional editorial values had the potential at least of breaking out of the mould of state-financed news organisations, which have been either too hamstrung by their financial and political masters to be balanced or too derivative of the CNN/BBC template to be original. AJE, like AJA, had the undoubted advantage of having a benefactor and bank-roller based in Qatar, which in theory at least gave it more editorial room for manœuvre. Qatar was never going to be a major story in the way that Putin's Russia or Chávez's Venezuela have attracted the world's attention. Secondly, the sheer size of its resources gave it much more freedom to choose its editorial focus as it could rely more on its own bureaux and less on what pictures happened to be available from APTN or Reuters.

But AJE clearly does have some similarities with Telesur in that it sees itself as providing news from the 'south'. It is interesting to note that in the early days, AJE's editorial perspective was not normally described by its Anglo-Saxon executives as 'Southern', and much less 'anti-Western'. However, the concept of the 'south' was used more volubly by the director-general of Al-Jazeera Networks, the Palestinian Wadah Khanfar. In September 2007, Khanfar presented AJE as 'the voice of the South', which meant in his view 'approaching the issues of the oppressed people and countries, regardless whether they were third world or advanced, noting that even advanced countries have their South'.[57] He further explained that this 'cultural and social South' existed all over the world and represented those whose voices are not heard through the main media channels. Khanfar believed that AJE 'filled the vacuum and expressed the soul of this south'.

Perhaps it was no coincidence that Wadah Khanfar should articulate such a non-Western vision of AJE to the Arab media at a time when reports continued to surface over the relative dominance of Westerners over

---

[56] <http://english.aljazeera.net/News/aspx/print.htm>.
[57] 'Al-Jazeera TV Chief Denies Split within Editorial Board', *Al-Safir* website, Beirut, <http://www.assafir.com> in Arabic (3 Sept. 2007), tr. BBC Monitoring.

non-Westerners amongst AJE's senior managerial and editorial staff.[58] But the important point is that a central strand of AJE's editorial thinking was focused on offering the 'voice of the south'. Even though he did not use the word 'south', the head of output at the Doha base John Pullman added a little more flesh to the concept. 'Our aim has been to cover people, those who are deprived, powerless and poor', he said.[59] He gave as examples Iraqi refugees in Germany, gypsies in Italy, immigrants in Malta and poverty in the USA, all of whom would no doubt fit the description of the 'cultural and social south'.

The concept of the 'south' is notoriously nebulous not least because the 'south' is often used as a catch-all term for developing countries when the political, economic, cultural and social differences between them can be just as great as those between advanced countries and developing countries. AJE was clearly not setting out to reflect what many observers see as a slow but fundamental shift in global power towards countries of the 'south', most notably China and India. If it had been, it would have set up at least one of its bases there. It was, though, attempting to get far more voices from the 'south' on air. But having more voices from the 'south' does not by itself guarantee a radical departure from a Western perspective. An interview with an Indian businessman may not offer a significantly different vision on the importance of free market policies to that of a Wall Street banker. The issue is of course 'which voices from the south?' Those of pro-Western governments in the south or only of those at odds with the West? Of rich southern elites or only the poor and down-trodden?

Khanfar's vision suggested a narrower sense of the 'voice of the voiceless and oppressed who do not normally get on the air', which puts greater emphasis on those who are suffering in the (cultural) 'south' rather than Southern elites. This is distinct from an editorial philosophy of giving more air time to the perspectives and experiences of developing countries compared to those of industrialised countries. The difference is important: putting suffering people of the world on air would hardly distinguish a channel from Oxfam's press office; putting experiences and perspectives of the 'south' on air is more in line with countering the 'Northern' or 'Western' bias of the BBC and CNN. The precise balance between portraying the suffering and perspectives of the developing world is at times a source of tension within AJE's overall editorial vision. But in general, AJE stops short of being a champion of the poor and sticks to its wider brief of viewing international events from a Southern perspective.

[58] Khanfar himself was reported to have lost his place on Al-Jazeera's board. See Ali Jaafar, 'Al-Jazeera Head Khanfar Loses Seat', *Variety* (6 July 2007).
[59] 'Al-Jazeera English Turns One', *Gulf Times*.

3 Testing the Difference

From the discussion above it is clear that a 'Southern' or 'non-Western' perspective could be tested in a variety of ways: in the selection of stories covered; in the time allocated to stories from the 'south' and in the place they appear in the running order compared to stories from the 'north'; in the amount of air time given to reactions from countries of the 'south' to major world events; in the manner of portrayal of people in the 'south' (passive victims of natural disasters or something else); in the amount of air time given to the voice of the voiceless of the 'south'; in the geographical location of the principal production bases; in the geographical distribution of news-gathering capacity; and in the ethnic mix of both management and staff positions.

A direct comparison with the output of CNNI and BBC World can offer some insights into some, but not all, of these issues. The two channels are seen as embodying a 'Western' perspective on news, to which AJE is in part reacting and against which it wants its editorial distinctiveness to be judged. Moreover, the two channels are by some way the market leaders amongst Anglophone international channels in most media markets of the world. Taking this into account, the following four hypotheses about AJE's news programmes seem a useful way of assessing both its editorial perspective and its distinctiveness:

(1) that in its coverage of international news, AJE pays more attention than BBCW and CNNI to stories whose main focus of attention concerns developing countries in Africa, Asia, the Middle East and Latin America in comparison to stories whose focus is the USA, Europe and other industrialised countries;

(2) that AJE in its treatment of major international news stories pays more attention to reactions from developing countries than its rivals;

(3) that AJE pays more attention than its rivals to under-reported areas of the world;

(4) that AJE in its news coverage of developing countries has a distinctive approach from CNNI and BBCW in that it presents more 'voices of the voiceless' and fewer politicians and experts.

The programmes monitored to test the above hypotheses were broadcast at different times and dates during 2007 and are outlined in the detailed discussions below. It should be stated at the outset that the sample taken may not be large enough to give a definitive answer to the hypotheses, but it is sufficient to suggest some trends. Also, the sample does not include any current affairs programmes, but only straight news programmes. AJE regularly broadcasts documentaries, talk shows and one-to-one interviews, often to be found in the back half hour of the hourly programme cycle. Flagship programmes such as *Witness*, *People and Power* and *Every Woman* strongly feature reports from developing countries. *Inside Iraq* and *101 East* obviously have a specifically regional focus.[60] However, it is worth stressing that news programmes make up about 45 per cent of all AJE's output. Secondly, AJE's news programmes are probably the most fruitful way of assessing any proclaimed editorial distinctiveness largely because they offer a more direct comparison with what rival channels are offering.

Testing hypothesis (1)

Even a cursory glance at the news output of AJE suggests that it is following a different editorial agenda to BBCW and CNNI. Examples abound, but a *locus classicus* could be seen at 0900 GMT on Tuesday 20 November 2007, when both BBCW and CNNI were leading their bulletins on the news that trade unions in France were stepping up their protests against the reform programme of President Sarkozy. A viewer of AJE on the other hand would have had to wait until twenty minutes into the bulletin to see a report from its correspondent in Paris on the strikes.[61] In other words, the editorial difference can lie just as much in the ordering as the choice of news stories.

At first sight, it seems that that AJE is – self-consciously or otherwise – downplaying or at times ignoring stories whose principal focus of attention is an event in an industrialised country. To test this thesis, several news programmes being broadcast at the same time by the three channels were

---

[60] In Oct. 2007, AJE's main long-format current affairs programmes were *101 East*, *Riz Khan*, *One on One*, *Frost Over the World*, *Listening Post*, *Inside Story*, *Inside Iraq*, *Talk to Al-Jazeera*, *Witness*, *People and Power* and *Every Woman*.

[61] This item came after stories on shootings in Iraq, prisoner releases in Pakistan, elections in Jordan, political deadlock in Beirut, hearings into the Khmer Rouge in Cambodia, and a meeting between the presidents of Venezuela and Iran.

monitored during the week starting Monday 26 November 2007 and ending on Sunday 2/Monday 3 December. Editorially, the week had a wide range of stories from different parts of the world including the Annapolis conference on the Middle East, the parliamentary elections in Russia, the referendum in Venezuela, the political crisis in Pakistan, the riots in Paris, a coup attempt in the Philippines and the arrest of a British teacher in Sudan. No one story dominated the agenda, although the Annapolis conference – the first in seven years on the Middle East – featured strongly in the early part of the week.

	AJE	BBCW	CNNI
26/11/2007 0900 GMT			
Programme	Newshour	BBC News	World News
Length monitored	30 minutes	30 minutes	30 minutes
27/11/2007 0900 GMT			
Programme	Newshour	BBC News	World News
Length monitored	30 minutes	30 minutes	30 Minutes
28/11/2007 0900 GMT			
Programme	Newshour	BBC News	World News
Length monitored	30 minutes	30 minutes	30 Minutes
29/11/2007 1900 GMT			
Programme	Riz Khan	World News Today	YW Today
Length monitored	5 minutes	30 minutes	30 minutes
30/11/2007 0900 GMT			
Programme	Newshour	BBC News	World News
Length monitored	30 minutes	30 minutes	15 minutes
3/12/2007 0000 GMT			
Programme	Newshour	BBC News	CNN Today
Length monitored:	30 minutes	30 minutes	30 minutes

Table 3.1. Programmes monitored

Table 3.1 shows the eighteen news programmes which were monitored, six from each channel, most of which lasted 30 minutes. As can be seen, priority was given to monitoring the channels at the same time to be able to compare like with like. 0900–0930 GMT was deemed a useful focus as all three channels broadcast a news programme at that time. BBCW and CNNI both run a programme of 30 minutes with the exception of Fridays, when CNNI shortens the programme to 15 minutes to be followed by the 15-minute programme *CNN Marketplace Middle East*. AJE's programme *Newshour* runs for 60 minutes but has a natural break after about 30 minutes for advertisements and channel promos.

As previously mentioned, AJE broadcasts from different production centres at different times of the days. This breaks down (roughly) into Kuala Lumpur 0400–0800 GMT, Doha 1100–1700, London 2000–2200 and Washington 2300–0200. At certain times it links its production centres, and 0900 is one of those times.[62] This means that at 0900 the channel is less 'regionally focused' than, for example, it clearly is at 0800 when it is broadcasting from Kuala Lumpur.(see below) CNNI also broadcasts from different centres at different times of the day, but at 0900 it is broadcasting from London, as is BBCW. All three channels target different regional audiences at different times of the day. So for example, BBCW in the afternoon hours of GMT tends to cover Asia, then in the evening hours of GMT Europe and the Middle East, and finally US later in the cycle. AJE's broadcast pattern from its four centres broadly follows this. The editorial decisions of all three channels partly reflect these priorities.

At 0900–0930 GMT on 29 November, all three channels were broadcasting live coverage of an attempted coup by rebel troops in the Philippines, using the same picture feed.[63] This was unsurprising given the imperative of any international 24/7 channel to broadcast live events unfolding. Because of the exceptional editorial nature of the programme at 0900, the programmes at 1900 GMT on the same day were monitored instead to give a better insight into the regional editorial priorities of the three channels. At that time, AJE broadcasts the *Riz Khan* show, but it includes a five-minute news round-up at the top of the programme. BBCW runs *World News Today* while CNNI broadcasts *Your World Today* (see Table 3.1). Finally, three

---

[62] AJE executives say three key editions of *Newshour* are at 0900, 1500 and 1800 GMT. The first links Doha and Kuala Lumpur, the second Doha and London, and the third Doha, London and Washington.
[63] AJE's coverage was arguably sharper than that of its rivals, not so much because of the location of its Kuala Lumpur base nearer to the action but because its main KL anchor, Veronica Pedrosa, is from the Philippines and worked for several years there as a correspondent. She was able to translate the press conferences being broadcast by the rebels and their supporters, and identify the main players.

programmes broadcast at 0000 GMT on Sunday 2/Monday 3 November were also monitored to include a wider range of programme times and days.

Each programme item was codified according to region and duration. Headlines, trails, teases, general promos, advertisements, sports and business coverage, and weather details were not included in the monitoring and were subtracted from the total amount of time so as to give a better comparison between the three channels of the percentage allocated to each region and story. The thorny issue of items that clearly covered two countries from different geographical areas was resolved in the following way. If the *principal* focus of attention was the story or fate of an individual or group of individuals from country X in country Y, then the story was classified as coming from country X. So, for example, the fate of the British teacher in Sudan who had let her class name a teddy bear Mohammed was initially classified as a UK story. If the item concerned the impact of the foreign policy of country X on country Y, then the times allocated were split equally between the two countries or regions in the coding. However, when considered appropriate, some of the stories were additionally codified in a different way to assess how much difference this made to the overall picture.

Table 3.2 shows the results. Most notably:

- AJE had significantly more coverage of events in developing countries than BBCW and CNNI: 81 per cent compared to 47 and 53 per cent respectively.
- AJE had significantly less coverage of Europe and the USA.
- AJE had significantly more coverage of the Middle East, whilst BBCW had more coverage of Europe and CNN had more coverage of the USA.

Table 3.3 shows that AJE's coverage of Europe drops further as a percentage of its overall coverage if Russia and Turkey are not classified as being parts of 'Europe'. Applying this criterion, only 8 per cent of AJE's coverage was of industrialised countries compared to 30 and 38 per cent respectively for BBCW and CNNI.

The three channels to a certain extent reflected their geographical homeland. AJE covered the Middle East the most of the three channels (42:19:25%), the BBC covered the UK more than the other two (0:10:9), whilst CNN covered the USA the most (1:1:20).[64]

The choice of headlines to a certain extent also reflected a geographical bias. AJE never headlined a story from the USA or Europe (assuming Russia

---

[64] However, other studies do show that BBCW has a much smaller percentage of domestic (UK) news compared to DeutscheWelle and EuroNews. See Robertson, 'Reporting the World Back to Itself', figure 1.

and Turkey are not part of Europe), whereas BBCW had three headlines from Europe, and CNNI had five from Europe and one from the USA.[65]

	AJE	BBCW	CNNI
Africa	7.50"	0.50"	0.00"
%	6	1	0
Asia	26.20"	20.30"	20.00"
%	19	17	19
Latin America	19.10"	11.30"	9.30"
%	14	10	9
Middle East	57.40"	23.10"	26.00"
%	42	19	25
Developing countries total	**81%**	**47%**	**53%**
Europe	23.00"	53.30"	20.50"
%	17	44	23
USA	1.50"	0.40"	21.40"
%	1	1	20
Other industrialised countries	1.00"	4.00"	0.50"
%	1	3	1
Industrialised countries total	**19%**	**48%**	**44%**
Other	0.00"	6.50"	3.10"
%	0	6	3
TOTAL	**100%**	**100%**	**100%**

Table 3.2. Coverage by region 1 (by number of minutes and %)

In the particular week monitored, none of the three channels devoted much attention to Africa, but AJE had the most (6:1:0). Most of the coverage of the arrest of the British teacher in Sudan was seen through the perspective of the fate of the teacher, the attempts to get her released, and the reactions in the UK. Indeed, CNNI covered the story out of London. However, as Table 3.4 shows, even if the times allocated are distributed equally between the UK and Africa instead of only to the UK, the overall picture of the balance between coverage of developing countries and industrialised countries does not change significantly.

---

[65] The sample was taken from the first three headlines at the top of the programmes, even though the three channels at times ran more than this number or ran 'teases' of other stories to be covered in the programme.

	AJE	BBCW	CNNI
Developing countries total	**81**	**47**	**53**
Europe without Russia/Turkey	6	26	17
USA	1	1	20
Other industrialised countries	1	3	1
Industrialised countries without Russia/Turkey	**8**	**30**	**38**
Russia	8	16	4
Turkey	3	2	2
Other	0	6	3
TOTAL	**100**	**100**	**100**

UK breakdown by number of minutes and percentage			
All UK stories	0.00"	2.20"	2.10"
UK teacher Sudan	0.40"	10.00"	7.40"
TOTAL	0.40"	12.20"	9.50"
%	0	10	9

Table 3.3. Coverage by region 2 (%)

Table 3.5 shows the seven stories that were covered most during the course of the week. Unsurprisingly, AJE ran the most on the Middle East conference and reactions to it (34:12:15), although a large part of the figure was made up of a long sequence of reactions in the programme on Wednesday 28 November. The BBC had the least coverage of the Middle East conference, but had significantly more coverage of the Russian elections and the Pakistan political crisis. The BBC had clearly decided to invest heavily in the deployment of considerable news-gathering capacity to Russia and Pakistan, both for BBC domestic outlets and BBC World.[66] CNN had the most coverage of the Venezuela referendum, perhaps reflecting US interest in the fate of President Chávez.[67] CNN also had the most time allocated to

---

[66] BBC World is often dependent to some extent for its coverage on the deployment of BBC correspondents for domestic consumption. Having a BBC correspondent in a certain place can of course drive editorial decisions about what to cover.

[67] It is of note that in the programmes monitored CNN gave considerable airtime to the protest movement in Venezuela, but much less to the government point of view. This may be due in part to CNN's limited access to government sources. On the night of the referendum (2 Dec.) AJE broadcast live coverage both from a pro-Chávez suburb of Caracas and from the 'no vote' headquarters, with correspondents in both locations.

the US elections as it was running almost daily reports on the standing of different candidates. It is worth pointing out that AJE did not play down the coverage of the Paris riots as might have been expected given its geographical location, perhaps because they involved marginalised 'powerless' sectors of French society.

	AJE	BBCW	CNNI
Africa	8.00"	5.50"	3.40"
%	6	5	3
Asia	26.20"	20.30"	20.00"
%	19	17	19
Lat. Am.	19.10"	11.30"	9.30"
%	14	10	9
M. East	57.40"	23.10"	26.00"
%	42	19	25
Developing countries total	**81%**	**51%**	**56%**
Europe	22.50"	48.30"	21.00"
%	17	40	20
USA	1.50"	0.40"	21.40"
%	1	1	20
Other industrialised countries	1.00"	4.00"	0.50"
%	1	3	1
Industrialised countries total	**19%**	**44%**	**41%**
Other	0.00"	6.50"	3.10"
%	0	6	3
TOTAL	**100%**	**100%**	**100%**

Table 3.4. Coverage by region 4 (by number of minutes and %)

But probably the most interesting difference is that of the relative weight given to the story of the British teacher Gillian Gibbons in Sudan. AJE virtually ignored it, as did her sister station AJA.[68] Rather, AJE ran two pieces during the week on the African Union mission in Darfur.[69] CNN and the BBC on the other hand ran detailed reports on the teacher story or

[68] An analysis of news programme summaries of AJA at 0400 GMT from 26 to 30 Nov. reveals no coverage of the teacher story. However, there were several items through the week on the situation in Darfur, the internal political situation in Sudan and the fighting in eastern Chad in which the Sudanese government is accused of arming rebel forces.

[69] AJE ran a third report on Darfur in the back 30 minutes of the *Newshour* programme at 0900 on 28 Nov., but this was not included as only the first 30 minutes were monitored in detail.

	AJE	BBCW	CNNI
Middle East conference/reactions	47.00"	14.50"	15.40"
%	34	12	15
Russian elections	12.10"	19.10"	4.30"
%	8	16	4
Pakistan political crisis	10.00"	16.00"	11.20"
%	7	13	11
Venezuela referendum	8.40"	2.00"	8.30"
%	6	2	8
Paris riots	5.20"	6.00"	3.20"
%	4	5	3
UK teacher/Sudan	0.40"	10.00"	7.40"
%	0	8	7
US elections	0.00"	0.00"	8.00"
%	0	0	8

Table 3.5. Coverage by topic (by number of minutes and %)

mentioned it in their news round-ups every day from Tuesday onwards. Indeed, it was a headline on CNNI three times, and on BBCW once. An inside source quoted in the *Guardian* newspaper suggested that AJE's deputy managing director had sent an email to staff 'banning the story ... because it would upset Muslims', and that the story only began to be covered when there riots in Sudan.[70] If this were the case, then clearly different editorial criteria are being brought to bear on stories beyond those discussed in this report.

Table 3.6 gives a breakdown of the amount of time allocated *on screen* to various protagonists or actors from Monday 26 November to Thursday 29 November during the coverage of the Annapolis conference and the reactions to it. Some caution should be applied before drawing any firm conclusions from the figures as *(a)* correspondents or in-house reporters can and did include an actor's point of view without there being pictures to illustrate it; *(b)* AJE had better access to a presence on the ground in Gaza than the BBC or CNN; and *(c)* all three channels ran extensive coverage of the story outside of the programmes monitored.

---

[70] Leigh Holmwood, 'Al-Jazeera English in "Staffing Crisis"', *Guardian* (30 Jan. 2008). The suggestion made by the source is that the AJE editor in question was 'pushing for the English channel to take a more Islamic slant'.

	Israelis	US officials	Palestinians	Gaza correspondent
AJE	3.50"	1.10"	13.10"	6.40"
	8%	2%	28%	14%
BBCW	1.55"	0.50"	2.20"	1.20"
	15%	6%	18%	10%
CNNI	1.50"	3.20"	1.00"	0.00"
	12%	21%	6%	0%

Notes: Israelis included government officials, negotiators, commentators and voices from the street; US officials included President Bush and government officials; Palestinians included negotiators, commentators, NGO representatives, Hamas officials and voices from the street. Percentage figures refer to amount of time of on-air pictures as a percentage of the total length of time allocated to reporting the story: in the case of AJE this was 47.00", BBCW 12.50", CNN 15.40".

Table 3.6. Coverage of Annapolis and reactions: time given to on-air pictures (with voices) of main actors

However, the differences between the three channels in the programmes monitored are still quite striking.

- All three channels gave a significant amount of time to the voices of Israelis, US officials and Palestinians. However, AJE included the most from Hamas, 50 seconds compared to 20 seconds from the BBC and none on CNN. AJE was the only one to include a clip of a Syrian official.
- AJE included a total of 13 minutes of Palestinian voices, compared to just one minute on CNN. This was largely due to a long sequence on 28 November which included 12 minutes of vox pops from Gaza, Ramallah and the Shatila refugee camp in Beirut, all mediated by different correspondents in each location.
- Expressed as percentages of the total duration of each station's coverage of the Annapolis conference and reactions to it, AJE had the largest proportion devoted to Palestinian voices: 28 per cent compared to 18 (BBCW) and 6 (CNNI).
- Both AJE and BBCW used correspondents in Gaza, although in the case of the BBC, this was by phone link-up where only the voice of the correspondent could be heard. Both correspondents dedicated a large part of their interview to giving the Palestinian point of view from the ground, which arguably could be counted as a Palestinian voice. In which case, the percentages allocated to Palestinian voices would be AJE 43 per cent, BBCW 28 per cent and CNNI 6 per cent.
- CNN had the highest percentage of time allocated to US voices: 21 per cent compared to 12 per cent (BBCW) and 6 per cent (AJE).

Finally, Table 3.7 shows the regional breakdown of stories from AJE's 0800 GMT 30-minute news programme from 4 to 10 December 2007.[71] This programme is broadcast from Kuala Lumpur, so as might be expected, there is a distinct geographical bias towards Asia at that time: 42 per cent of the programmes covered Asian stories compared to 19 per cent at 0900 GMT in the programmes monitored from Monday 26 November onwards. Percentage figures for Africa (10:6), Latin America (14:7) and Europe (7:8) are not that different between the two weeks concerned. The most significant variations are between the figures for the Middle East (17:42) and the United States (14:1). However, in the case of the figure for the Middle East, there was no one big story in the week 4–10 December to compare with the Annapolis peace conference. And in the case of the United States, most of the coverage during the second week was of US relations with different developing countries, which results in a relatively high figure due to the methodology being used. If the US figure was restricted just to stories where the only focus of attention was the US, it would drop to just 6 per cent.

	4 Dec.	5 Dec.	6 Dec.	7 Dec.	8 Dec.	9 Dec.	10 Dec.	Totals
Africa	3.15"	2.00"	6.00"	5.00"	1.30"	0.15"	0.00"	**18.00"** 10%
Asia	12.15"	12.00"	7.00"	6.30"	12.00"	17.00"	6.30"	**73.15"** 42%
Lat. Am	0.00"	0.00"	0.00"	6.00"	3.00"	0.00"	3.00"	**12.00"** 7%
M. East	7.15"	6.00"	6.00"	1.30"	1.30"	3.30"	3.00"	**28.45"** 17%
Europe	1.15"	0.00"	0.00"	0.00"	5.00"	0.15"	6.00"	**12.30"** 7%
USA	2.15"	6.50"	3.00"	5.30"	1.30"	1.30"	3.30"	**24.05"** 14%
Other industr'd countries	0.15"	0.00"	0.00"	0.00"	0.00"	0.30"	0.00"	**0.45"** 0%
Other	0.00"	0.00"	3.00"	0.00"	0.30"	0.30"	0.00"	**4.00"** 2%
TOTAL	26.30"	26.50"	25.00"	24.30"	25.00"	23.30"	22.00"	**173.20"** 100%

Table 3.7. Coverage by region, AJE, 4–10 December 2007, 0800 GMT
(by number of minutes and %)

[71] The source is the programme summaries of Al-Jazeera English supplied by BBC Monitoring.

Table 3.7 is important for several reasons. First, it expands the sample size for AJE beyond the programmes analysed in Tables 3.2 to 3.6. This second sample does strongly support the view that industrialised countries do receive much less attention than developing countries in a proportion of 21:76 per cent.[72] Again, this is not that dissimilar to the more detailed sample from 26 November onwards (19:81). Not surprisingly, it also suggests AJE does pay more attention to the stories to the region where its main regional hub is based at the time of broadcasting. This strengthens the view that 0900 GMT is a useful time to monitor in detail as the AJE programme has a less regional-specific bias at that time. But it also suggests that more content analysis would have to be done from AJE's other regional hubs to have a more complete picture of any regional favouritism in its overall coverage.

Finally, it is worth making a brief mention of the three channels' coverage of business stories. BBCW has a regular slot in many of its news programme, including its 0900 edition, which usually lasts about two minutes. In the week in question, virtually all the stories covered were from the industrialised world in the sample monitored. This of course would have further inflated the percentage figures for coverage of the industrialised world. CNN has a series of business programmes throughout its schedules, and runs a round-up of world markets on screen during the 0900 programmes monitored. AJE in contrast has no coverage of business in its first half hour at 0900, but it does have a one-minute round-up of world stock markets, exchange rates and commodity prices towards the end of the second half hour within a commercial break. In general, AJE has no specific business programmes, though this is expected to change after the appointment of a new programming director in late 2007.[73]

Testing hypothesis (2)

A useful case study for testing hypothesis (2) is 6 April 2007. On that day, there were two strong international stories: the press conference given on the day after their return to the UK by some of the fifteen British sailors and marines captured by the Iranian navy two weeks previously; and the release of the report by the Intergovernmental Panel on Climate Change (IPCC) on 'Impacts, Adaptation and Vulnerability'.

At 1800 GMT (AJE and BBCW) and at 1700 GMT (CNNI), all three channels chose to lead with the press conference as their first headline, followed by the IPCC report as their second headline. Moreover, all three

[72] The missing 3% is made up of other stories, in this case mostly on climate change.
[73] Ali Jaafar, 'Al-Jazeera English Shows Mixed Results', *Variety* (25 Sept. 2007).

channels were almost identical in dedicating most of the first nine minutes of their news programme to the Iran–UK incident, before switching to their coverage of the IPCC report. Table 3.8 gives the headlines of all three programmes and the amount of time allocated to the two main stories in the first half hour of the programme.

	Headlines
AJE	UK sailors back from Iran
	IPCC report
	Trail forward to two features on climate change
BBCW	UK sailors back from Iran
	IPCC report
	Trail forward to feature on the Ganges
CNNI	UK sailors back from Iran
	IPCC report
	Trail forward to feature on plastic bags in India

	Major items in first 30 minutes	Time allocated
AJE	1. UK sailors press conference	7.00"
	2. IPCC report and climate change	13.30"
BBCW	1. UK sailors press conference	7.30"
	2. IPCC report and climate change	5.40"
CNNI	1. UK sailors press conference	16.30"
	2. IPCC report and climate change	4.00"

Table 3.8. Overview of programme content of AJE, BBCW and CNNI (6 April 2007)

As can be observed, the three channels ran the same first two headlines and assigned a very significant portion of the first half hour of their programmes to the two stories.[74] However, even though the editorial weight both in terms of the running order and the volume of coverage assigned to the two stories was roughly similar, the treatment of both stories shows interesting differences of approach.

---

[74] BBCW's total of fewer minutes is largely explained by the programme having fixed economy, sports and weather slots and longer commercial breaks which accounted for about 10 minutes in total.

Treatment of UK–Iran story

An analysis of the transcripts and summaries of the coverage of the UK service personnel's press conference[75] would suggest the following observations. First, all three channels included Iran's reaction to the press conference, which was essentially that it had been stage-managed for propaganda purposes by the British military/government. BBCW mentioned the reaction in the introduction to their whole sequence, whereas AJE included it in their in-house report. CNNI included discussion of it by their presenters after showing an uninterrupted repeat of about 15 minutes of the press conference. Both AJE and BBCW went live to Tehran at the end of their sequences for interviews lasting about 2.30 minutes. CNNI's discussion of Iran's reaction in contrast only lasted about 1.20 minutes, but it did not have the option of going to Tehran due to the absence of a CNN bureau there.

Second, AJE's interviewee in Tehran was an Iranian political analyst from Tehran University, Seyed Mohammad Marandi, whereas the BBCW's interviewee was the BBC correspondent there, Frances Harrison. Ms Harrison essentially gave a straight report of what the Iranian government and media were saying, whereas Mr Marandi advanced a series of arguments as to why the Iranian government and Iranians in general would think the press conference was stage-managed (namely, the sailors had been debriefed by the British military, the conference was not spontaneous, and they were reading from a prepared text). He certainly gave the viewer more understanding of the Iranian stance, but in effect his analysis was little different to that of a spokesman for the government.

Third, AJE's framing of their coverage was different to that of BBCW and CNNI. For example, both BBCW and AJE ran the same clip in the headlines of a UK sailor talking of the conditions of their detention, but AJE immediately stressed that what the UK service personnel were saying at the conference was a different version of what they had said while in Iran. The theme of there being two different stories was developed in the presenter's introduction, and mentioned in their in-house report. The BBC hinted at the context for the news conference by using such phrases as 'following a thorough debriefing' and 'in a prepared statement about what happened', but did not spell out in the same way as AJE that an essential part of the story was that the two governments were trying to get across their version of events. CNNI chose to open their coverage with the British troops' account of what happened when they were captured and how they

[75] Transcripts are available on the RISJ website at
<http://reutersinstitute.politics.ox.ac.uk/counterhegemonicnews.html>.

were treated under detention. A viewer of CNNI had to wait a long time (until the twenty-seventh minute of the programme) to hear the reaction from the Iranian government, followed by the suggestion that both governments were involved in a propaganda battle.

Fourth, AJE raised the question right at the beginning of their sequence in the headlines read by the presenter as to whether Iran had done anything wrong. The same question was reinforced at the end of the sequence. The presenter said textually 'So the question remains, who was in the right? Did Iran do anything wrong?' This was also used as a trail forward to an interview with an expert in international law in the second half of the programme.

In conclusion, none of the three channels were completely partisan in their coverage. All three included the Iranian reaction, the Iranian view that the UK service personnel were captured in Iranian waters and the observation that they had not been physically harmed. A more thorough analysis of the language and imagery of the reports would give a fuller picture of the treatment of the story. But there is enough evidence outlined in the four points here to conclude that, whereas all three channels showed some degree of balance, AJE's coverage gave more weight than the other channels to a (quasi-) Iranian government point of view.

Treatment of the IPCC report

As can be seen from Table 3.8 above, all three channels dedicated a considerable portion of their programme to the IPCC report, known in full as the Fourth Assessment Report, Working Group II, on 'Impacts, Adaptation and Vulnerability'. The report focused particularly on how the poor in developing countries would probably be the worst hit from drought, floods and storms. It pin-pointed four areas of particular concern: the Asian mega-deltas, sub-Saharan Africa, small islands and Arctic regions. An examination of the coverage by the three channels suggests the following conclusions:[76]

• AJE allocated more than twice the amount of time than the other two channels to their coverage of the report and the general topic of climate change.
• All three channels focused on the impact of climate change on developing countries or illustrated the general problem with examples from developing countries. However, AJE included more aspects to the story by including the debate on the IPCC report which in part covered the issue of the impact on developing countries and what countries like India and China should

[76] For a full breakdown of the programmes, see Painter, 'All Doom and Gloom', appendix 2.

do to combat the effects of climate change. It also included more discussion of possible solutions: the report from China mentioned what steps the country was taking to develop alternative energy sources, and the feature from London showed how scientists in the UK were developing a way of capturing the energy left by footsteps.

- None of the three channels included reaction to the IPCC report from a developing country, which might have been expected given the main message of the report. It was notable that AJE's debate was between two Western experts.
- There was only one voice from Africa in the whole of the coverage by the three channels. This was a prerecorded clip in the CNNI in-house report by Grace Akumu, of the Climate Network Africa, about Africans suffering more than was fair. This was despite the fact that the IPCC report highlighted sub-Saharan Africa as one of the four main areas to be hit hardest.
- In the coverage of all three channels, there were no 'voices of the voiceless', or of the poor who are being, or will be, most affected by climate change. In contrast, several voices of experts were included.

In conclusion, AJE's coverage stood out in the particular programmes monitored for being more comprehensive, but did not stand out for putting on air more reactions to the report from developing countries or for including new types of voices from those countries.

Testing hypothesis (3)

In its promotional material, both on and off-screen, AJE stresses it reports on, and from, under-reported areas of the world. It is not always clear which countries or regions it regards as fitting this category, but it would be safe to include Myanmar, Somalia, Sudan, Zimbabwe and the Democratic Republic of Congo (DRC). Afghanistan is also often mentioned. Both CNNI and the BBC have permanent correspondents there, but AJE stresses that it does more reporting on life in the country as opposed to reports based on accompanying Western troops. Certainly in the early days, AJE paraded its correspondents in some parts of the world where the BBC was either banned (Zimbabwe) or had constant problems of access (Darfur).[77]

In the programmes monitored from 26 November to 3 December, Sudan was the only country of those listed above to feature in AJE's output. In all, AJE ran about 7.50 minutes of coverage of Sudan, consisting of two

[77] On the very first day of AJE's broadcasting, at 1200 GMT 15 Nov. 2006, the running order was Gaza, Darfur, Iran, Zimbabwe.

features on Darfur, and three short news items on Darfur, relations between Sudan and Chad, and the UK teacher in jail. If the item on the British teacher is excluded, this leaves a total of 7.20 minutes, of which 6.50 minutes was on Darfur and 0.30 on Sudan and Chad: 6.50 minutes represents about 5 per cent of all AJE's monitored output that week, compared to BBCW's 0.20 per cent on Sudan, and nothing on CNNI. This 5 per cent figure is less than the BBC and CNN dedicated to covering the fate of the UK teacher (8 and 7 per cent respectively), but more than AJE assigned to the Paris riots.[78]

But a note of caution is in order. *At times*, AJE does follow a remarkably similar news agenda to BBCW in particular, covering the same stories from 'under-reported parts of the world', and indeed, providing a similar treatment of those stories. The night of 27/28 October 2007 at 0000 GMT is a case in point. Darfur, Somalia and Afghanistan all featured in the news that day. At the time in question, both BBCW and AJE broadcast a short news summary lasting 4.30 minutes.[79] As can be seen from Table 3.9, the news agendas of the two channels were very similar. Moreover, both channels had a very similar treatment of the lead story, namely the Darfur

	Item	Length	Nature of report
BBC	Talks on Darfur	1.45"	Correspondent in Libya
	Killings in Somalia	1.45"	In-house report
	Bhutto to ancestral home	0.20"	Presenter with pix
	Fighting in Afghanistan	0.20"	Presenter with pix
AJE	Talks on Darfur	2.45"	Correspondent in Libya
	Killings in Somalia	0.15"	Presenter with pix
	Fighting in Afghanistan	0.15"	Presenter with pix
	Flooding in DRC	0.15"	Presenter with pix
	Argentina elections	0.30"	Presenter with pix

Table 3.9. AJE and BBCW programmes at 0000 GMT 28 October 2007

[78] In the week 4–10 Dec. at 0800 GMT, AJE ran one three-minute report each on Somalia, DRC and Sudan, and mentioned Myanmar in four of the seven programmes (two reports and four short news items). Unfortunately, it is not known how this compares with BBCW and CNNI, but it would be surprising if either channel had as much coverage.
[79] CNNI does not provide a useful base of comparison at that time, as it runs a 30 minute programme called *World News*. However, it is worth pointing out CNNI's different editorial priorities: first, the Darfur peace talks and the fighting in Somalia appear further down the running order after ten minutes of the programme, and are presented only in short summary form of about 20 seconds each. Longer reports on Benazir Bhutto's return to her ancestral home, the diplomacy between Turkey and Iraq over the Kurds in northern Iraq and a situation report on village in Iraq all appeared first. Secondly, a four-minute sequence on the fires in California was included in the first half of the programme, a story ignored at that time by both BBCW and AJE.

peace talks taking place in the Libyan town of Sirte. The two channels had a correspondent at the talks, so a comparison is helpful.

The main essence of the story was similar on both channels. The two correspondents, Jonah Fisher of the BBC and Mohammed Adow of AJE, stressed several similar aspects, namely: the talks got off to a bad start due to the absence of some of the key rebel leaders from Darfur; the disappointment expressed by the host of the talks, Muammar Gaddafi; a unilateral ceasefire announced by the Sudanese government rebels; the optimism of the UN envoy, Jan Eliasson, about the future of the talks; and the analysis that the talks were not going to bring a resolution to the four-year conflict without the participation of the main Darfuri rebel leaders in the future. Mohammed Adow's report included a little more historical context and the reaction from the rebel leaders present to the government announcement of a unilateral ceasefire. But this could in part be ascribed to the longer duration of his report (by one minute).

It could be argued with some justification that a short report on peace talks in Sudan should not be seen as too representative of a wider trend, particularly when the news elements were self-evident. It may also be of significance that Mohammed Adow had eight years' experience of working for the BBC in East Africa before joining AJE, which could be a factor in accounting for the similarity of treatment.

However, this example should serve as a counter-weight to any simplistic view that AJE will always include more stories from under-reported parts of the world than the BBC and CNN, or that when it is covering a story from an 'under-reported country', it will offer a different treatment. It also shows that the employment of a correspondent from the region is no guarantee by itself of a different perspective on the news from that of an Anglo-Saxon correspondent.

Testing hypothesis (4)

It has already been shown that there is considerable evidence to suggest that AJE downplays the importance of stories about the developed world in favour of the developing world. It is also the case that AJE rarely – if ever – runs stories about royalty or celebrities from the developed world in its news programmes. Examples abound,[80] but suffice it to say that on 19 November 2007 for example, it ran no coverage of the diamond (sixtieth)

---

[80] AJE ignored the first press conference of the footballer David Beckham in Los Angeles on 13 July 2007, which BBCW carried live. It prides itself on ignoring such celebrities as Paris Hilton and Lindsay Lohan.

wedding anniversary celebrations of the Queen and Prince Philip. BBCW on the other hand headlined the story.

So does AJE include in its news programmes more voices of ordinary people, the 'powerless' or the 'oppressed'? As discussed above, it was notable that AJE's coverage of the IPCC report on 6 April in the programme monitored did *not* stand out for including voices of ordinary people from the south. However, a more detailed monitoring of the three channels' coverage of the Annapolis conference does suggest that at other times AJE has included more voices of ordinary people, but not necessarily at the expense of experts or politicians.

Table 3.10 shows that AJE had by far the greatest amount of time devoted to vox pops (nearly sixteen minutes compared to just over a minute from the BBC and none from CNN), and by far the largest number of different voices (13:1:0). Of these, by far the largest amount of time (12.25 minutes) was given over to Palestinians and the largest number of voices (11) was those of Palestinians. AJE had the least amount of time devoted to experts and officials (even though it had a much larger total of time assigned to coverage of the Annapolis conference), but roughly the same number of voices. So, there is some initial evidence for arguing that AJE is presenting more voices of the voiceless (in this case the Palestinians), but not necessarily fewer politicians and experts.

	AJE	BBCW	CNNI
Vox pops			
Israelis	3.25" (2)	1.15" (1)	0.0"
Palestinians	12.25"(11)	0.0"	0.0"
Total	**15.50"(13)**	**1.15"(1)**	**0.0"**
Gov. officials and negotiators			
Israelis	0.25" (2)	0.40" (3)	1.10"(4)
US	1.10" (3)	0.50" (3)	3.20" (4)
Palestinians	0.45"(2)	0.20" (1)	0.40" (3)
Syrian	0.10" (1)	0.0"	0.0"
Hamas	0.50" (2)	0.20" (1)	0.0"
Experts/NGOs			
Israelis	0.0"	0.0"	0.40" (2)
Palestinians	0.0"	1.40" (1)	0.20" (1)
TOTAL	**3.20" (10)**	**3.50"(9)**	**6.10" (14)**

Table 3.10. Voices from the Middle East (by numbers of minutes and of voices)

Again, a note of caution is in order. It could be argued that AJE's coverage of the Annapolis conference is not sufficiently representative because *(a)* the figures are distorted by AJE's long sequence on 28 November of voices from Gaza, Ramallah and Lebanon; *(b)* unlike CNNI and BBCW, it has the resources and access to put such voices on air; and *(c)* it would be surprising if AJE had not included so many voices of this type when it had such a large overall total of minutes of coverage in comparison to the other two channels. More analysis of other news programmes is needed.[81]

Conclusions

On the basis of the news programmes monitored above, there is little evidence to suggest that AJE is following an overtly partisan agenda in the way in which, as will be seen in the next two chapters, Telesur may be perceived to be doing. Most stories have some degree of balance. In terms of its editorial perspective, the following conclusions can be drawn:

(1) There is considerable evidence to suggest that in comparison to BBCW and CNNI, AJE has significantly more coverage of events in developing countries and significantly less coverage of Europe and the USA.

(2) There is strong evidence to suggest that like BBCW and CNNI, AJE covers its 'geographical homeland' (the Middle East) more than the other two channels.

(3) There is some evidence to suggest that AJE at times seeks more reaction to major international stories from developing countries, particularly in the case of Iran, but at other times this is not the case.

(4) There is considerable evidence to suggest that AJE covers 'under-reported' parts of the world more than its rivals, and in particular events in Sudan. There is considerable difference between AJE and the other channels as to what constitutes a story about Sudan. However, at times the *treatment* of stories out of those countries does not differ widely.

(5) There is some evidence to suggest that AJE includes more voices of the voiceless, and particularly the voices of the Palestinians, but not necessarily fewer politicians and experts.

---

[81] A comparison of the coverage of the Venezuela referendum at 0000 GMT on 3 Dec. 2007 would suggest that AJE had slightly more voices from the street than BBCW and CNNI, but the sample is very small. In their reports at that time, AJE had two vox pops, the BBC one and CNN none. All three included the voice of one politician (Hugo Chávez).

4 The Arrival of Telesur

It is not journalistic hyperbole to describe 24 July 2005 as a historic date in the evolution of Latin American television. It was the day Telesur launched four hours of programming, to expand to 24 hours a day in October that year. President Hugo Chávez was attempting to reverse years of private-sector TV domination in Latin America by investing millions of dollars of state money in a new TV channel.[82] It was the first government-funded round-the-clock news and information channel based in a Latin American country with regional news agenda.

Telesur as public diplomacy

Telesur's genesis cannot be understood outside of the political context of Venezuela and its relations with the United States. Two of its fundamental aims were born out of Chávez's desire to promote the integration of Latin America and to confront the Bush administration.[83] One of the main reasons he has spent so much time travelling within and outside Latin America is his attempt to create a common ideological front against President Bush and to project his international standing as the leader of the anti-Bush forces. His aggressive stance is rooted in a sense of outrage at what he sees as international injustice – such as the war in Iraq, the political and economic domination of US interests, an unjust world order and the situation of the Palestinians.

[82] For a full discussion of the domination of private sector television and the weakness of state sector media in Latin America, see James Painter, 'The Boom in Counter-Hegemonic News Channels: A Case Study of Telesur', research paper presented to the Reuters Institute for the Study of Journalism (RISJ), Oxford, Feb. 2007, ch. 3, available at http://reutersinstitute.politics.ox.ac.uk/fileadmin/documents/James_Painter.pdf>; Elizabeth Fox and Silvio Waisbord (eds), *Latin Politics, Global Media* (Austin, Tex.: University of Texas Press, 2002), and John Sinclair, *Latin American Television: A Global View* (Oxford: OUP, 1999).
[83] A useful critique of these two fundamental aims can be found in Andrés Cañizález and Jairo Lugo, 'Telesur: Estrategia geopolítica con fines integracionistas', *CONfines* (Aug.–Dec. 2007).

Within Latin America, he wants to cast himself as the spokesman for a region more integrated economically and, more importantly, united politically against Washington's influence. His highly publicised invectives against President Bush have given Venezuela an influence and status way beyond its historical international profile. Telesur is one of several regional institutions set up to combat US cultural and economic domination. They include Bancosur (a regional development bank to counter the IMF and World Bank) and the trading bloc called ALBA (the Bolivarian alternative for the Americas) to counter the Bush administration's free trade agreements. As such, Telesur is in part an exercise in public diplomacy in order to project an active and muscular foreign policy that is anti-Bush, pro-integration and anti-free trade.

Chávez has used his windfall oil revenues to try to spread his ideas and bolster his leadership amongst the various left-wing governments that have been sweeping much of the region in recent years. The term 'left-wing' hides a multiplicity of regime types, which have varied in their desire to stand up publicly to Washington, their approach towards foreign investment, and the radicalism of their rhetoric. Chávez's '21st century socialism' has counted on strong support from Presidents Evo Morales in Bolivia, Fidel Castro in Cuba, Daniel Ortega in Nicaragua and Rafael Correa in Ecuador. However, other left-leaning governments, such as Presidents Bachelet in Chile and Lula in Brazil, have been reluctant to accept Chávez as the continent's left-wing leader. Very few governments in Latin America have rejected his economic largesse, but few too have embraced his regional projects.[84]

Chávez's trips outside Latin America have taken in most parts of the world, including China, Russia, India, the Middle East and several African countries. In part, his motives are to diversify Venezuela's historical dependence on the US for oil markets, arms sales, trade and investment. But he is also keen to cock a snook at Washington by parading close relationships with regimes that are anathema to the Bush administration. President Ahmadinejad's Iran and President Lukashenko's Belarus formed part of his July 2006 tour. North Korea was taken off the itinerary at a late stage. Previously he was one of only a handful of presidents to visit Saddam Hussein's Iraq. Most notably, Venezuela has been one of the very few countries to consistently vote in favour of Iran's nuclear energy programme at UN fora.

---

[84] For a critique of the impact of his regional projects, see Joseph Contreras, 'The Ghost of Simón Bolívar', *Newsweek* (14 Jan. 2008).

He has spent millions of dollars on arms deals with Russia, provided London's former Mayor, Ken Livingstone, with subsidised petrol for London buses, given subsidised heating oil to poor communities in cities in the USA and offered modest amounts of aid to four African countries. In January 2007 Chávez and President Ahmadinejad of Iran announced a joint US$2bn fund to help development projects, mainly in Latin America and Africa, to 'allow governments to free themselves from the imperialist yoke of the United States'. On the first anniversary of Telesur, President Chávez proposed to the 53 members of the African Union that they should join the Telesur network to improve integration between Latin America and Africa. It was symbolic of the meshing of his media and foreign policy aims. Telesur fits the pattern of Chávez using his petrodollars to spread his message and influence beyond Venezuela. It is in part an exercise in international relations similar to the function of Russia Today, CCTV-9 or Press TV.

Telesur: levelling the playing field

The other essential context for understanding Telesur is the battle within Venezuela over control over the media. The two worlds of Venezuelan politics and Venezuelan media have at times been so intertwined that it is hard to discuss them as separate entities. In the period between the run-up to the failed coup against Chávez in April 2002 and the end of 2005, the privately owned media filled the gap left by the political parties and took over as the main, and at times the only, opposition to Chávez.

The media opposition was initially led by two TV stations, Venevisión and RCTV (Radio Caracas Television), which in recent years have held a dominant share of the market. In the early 2000s, this was variously estimated at between 60 and 80 per cent.[85] Two other privately owned stations, Globovisión and Televen, make up the other two members of the group of four terrestrial channels Chávez liked to demonise as the 'four horses of the Apocalypse'.[86] Like previous governments, Chávez could count on the support of the state TV channel VTV, but this had historically suffered from low audience ratings.

By 2002 private-sector media coverage was openly siding with opposition political parties and civic groups. Their explanation was that

---

[85] John Sinclair, "The Globalization of Latin Media", *NACLA* 37/4 (Jan.–Feb. 2004), 19, and C. Lawson and S. Hughes, 'Latin America's Postauthoritarian Media', in A.K. Milton and R. May (eds) *Uncivil Societies: Human Rights and Democratic Transitions in Eastern Europe and Latin America* (Lanham Md.: Lexington, 2005), pp. 177.

[86] Phil Gunson, 'Venezuela's Media in a Bolivarian Storm'', *openDemocracy* (7 Aug. 2006).

they had to resist Chávez's stewardship of the country, which they saw as leading to a form of Castro-like communism. Starting in March 2002, the opposition began a series of huge anti-Chávez marches, to which the four main stations gave blanket coverage, while downplaying or at times ignoring the pro-Chávez response. In their coverage of the failed coup attempt on 11 April and after, the same four stations were wholly selective of what they decided to cover, in effect supporting the coup. They initially encouraged Venezuelans to join a large anti-Chávez march. Then they failed to cover the pro-Chávez riots and protests, the collapse of the short-lived Carmona regime, and Chávez supporters taking control of the presidential palace. Despite the failure of the coup attempt, the protests continued with a two-month long national strike, an oil production stoppage, and a recall referendum in August 2004 (which Chávez won).[87]

From 1999 to the start of 2007, Chávez chose not to shut down the opposition media – much to the surprise of some of his supporters. Freedom of expression continued, on the whole, there was seldom any overt censorship, and unlike in Cuba, journalists were not imprisoned for long periods for criticising his regime. However, he aimed to neutralise their influence by passing restrictive laws and promoting state-funded media to correct the asymmetry of market domination by the oligopoly of private companies. The use of oil money to fund Telesur was part of the effort to level the media playing field, albeit over a wider ambit of operations than Venezuela.

In addition to Telesur, Chávez purchased or increased state investment in five TV channels, eight federal and regional radio stations, a government news agency with a special media monitoring unit, and community TV and radio. Official figures are not available for the levels of investment but some put it as high as US$56m. It amounted to an 'alternative media empire' in the words of leading critic Teodoro Petkoff, who saw it as part of Chávez becoming a 'Caribbean Gramsci' and occupying 'the intermediary bodies in society' such as sports institutions, educational establishments and the media.[88]

Telesur: 'our north is the south'

Telesur was always promoted as a regional and not a Venezuelan channel, with important participation from different left-wing governments in Latin

---

[87] Much of the opposition continues to regard the result as fraudulent, partly because of the partisan behaviour of the National Electoral Council (CNE) in the pre-referendum period.
[88] Quoted in 'Chávez Heading towards "Totalitarianism Lite"', *El Pais* website, <http://www.elpais.com> (26 Dec. 2006), tr. BBC Monitoring.

America. At the outset, the Venezuelan government had the largest stake at 70 per cent, with Argentina 20 per cent and Uruguay 10 per cent. Over the next two years, the Venezuelan stake decreased in order to include participation from Bolivia, Cuba, Nicaragua and Ecuador.

The Cuban and Argentinian authorities provided some in-country logistical support for correspondents, but the actual funding came from the Venezuelan government, the Venezuelan state oil company PDVSA and the Venezuelan Mining Ministry. The budget was widely reported to be US$2.5m in start-up costs and about US$10m for the first year's running costs. Telesur's first president, Andrés Izarra, estimates the channel needs an annual budget of US$15–20m.[89]

Before its launch Telesur's directors claimed it was not going to be a propaganda station. Rather, it would be a 'public service not dissimilar to the BBC' which offered balanced and pluralistic coverage in its news. But from the outset there was plenty of fodder for those who wanted to dismiss the new channel as left-wing propaganda. Its advertisements were not commercials but a mixture of self-publicity, public service announcements and spots stressing the success of the Venezuelan and Cuban governments' social programmes. Its profile of documentaries seemed to be replete with nostalgic treatments of left-wing leaders,[90] while its international advisory board consisted of several high-profile left-wing intellectuals like the British Pakistani, Tariq Ali, and the Uruguayan writer, Eduardo Galeano.[91] Editions of its round table discussion programme, *Mesa Redonda*, seemed to be populated by like-minded pundits. Critics also pointed to the Izarra's appointment as president of the channel when he had previously been Chávez's minister of information, and to Telesur's location in the same grounds as Venezuela's state-run TV station, channel 8.[92]

Telesur's directors were keen to stress what they loosely called its 'Latin American integrationist' view and one which 'reflected Latin America's diversity'. This meant in practice an emphasis on detailed Latin American news so 'Latin Americans can know themselves better'.[93] One of the first publicity spots depicted several people being asked to name the capital of France. All of them get it right, but when they are asked to name the capital

---

[89] Author interview, Andrés Izarra (30 Oct. 2006).
[90] News accounts for about 40% of programming, while the remainder is made up of documentaries, round-table discussions, films and cultural programmes.
[91] For a fuller description of its documentaries and members of the board, see Nikolas Kozloff, *Hugo Chávez: Oil, Politics, and the Challenge to the U.S.* (New York: Palgrave Macmillan, 2006), pp. 126–7.
[92] Gary Marx, 'Will Truth Go South on Telesur News?', *Chicago Tribune* (17 July 2005).
[93] Interview with Andrés Izarra, 'Telesur es una ventana al acontecer latinoamericano', published in *Causa Popular* (Buenos Aires, 21 Jan. 2006), <www.causapopular.com.ar/article794.html>.

of Honduras, only one knows the answer (Tegucigalpa). 'Let's get to know each other', ends the slot.

Its emphasis on offering a greater range of Latin American stories was underpinned logistically and financially by its news-gathering efforts. It enjoyed an extensive news-gathering capacity – probably the most comprehensive of any Latin American media group working in the region. In early 2007 it had ten bureaux (Caracas, La Paz, Buenos Aires, Washington, Havana, Managua, Bogota, Brasilia, Mexico City and Port-au-Prince) with plans for three more in Latin America (Lima, Quito and Montevideo), and possibly for their first one outside the Americas somewhere in Europe. There is no doubt that the range of stories it covers compares favourably with any of its television competitors. Its main newscast, *Telesur Noticias*, is usually dedicated to a wide number of stories from Latin America. This means that it can and does offer themes that are not often seen on other channels in such depth.

In the months that followed its launch, it consolidated its multimedia offer. Telesur's priority is clearly the 24/7 TV operation, but it boasts a website (http://www.telesurtv.net/) regularly updated with news in text, and on demand and live video features. In September 2006 it announced a new press agency to compete with Reuters and Associated Press, and early in 2007 a multinational network of state radio stations, Radiosur, as 'an alternative to the large radio stations owned by big corporations'.[94]

Telesur clearly set itself up to be counter-hegemonic in the sense of offering a different vision or news content to the main Western media like CNN and the BBC. Its directors in public expressed their respect for CNN but were keen to stress the differences. CNN was described as being 'shaped by US interests, US culture and a US view of the world'. CNN en español is by some margin the market leader in international TV news in the region for those who want to find an alternative to the international news coverage provided by national TV stations.[95] It should be no surprise then that a key element of Telesur's rationale was to compete with CNN, although not necessarily aiming for the same target audience.

Telesur's pithy slogan, 'our north is the south', embodied another element of its counter-hegemonic approach. It saw itself as an alternative voice to CNN, providing news from the south (Latin America) seen through Latin

[94] Matilde Sosa, 'Nacerá la hermana radial de Telesur', *Argenpress* (4 Jan. 2007).
[95] Market figures suggest that CNN en español is the only major 24-hour international news channel with a consistently high reach across various Latin American countries. In 2002 it had a weekly audience of 12.8 million in Latin America in Spanish (and 4.4 million in English for CNN International). Most other international broadcasters, including the BBC, RAI, TVE, Deutsche Welle and Telemundo, were 'niche players' with usually between one and two million viewers each.

American eyes, in contrast to CNN's base in Atlanta in the north (the USA). Its directors are fond of portraying it as an antidote to the 'information imperialism' of Western media and big corporations, whereby the dominant news flow is from the 'West to the rest'. Articles lauding Telesur stressed how Latin American television has long been dominated by TV programming, films and music originating outside of the region and in particular from the USA.[96] It also sees itself as 'alternative' by providing air time to those voices (particularly from social movements) and themes which are usually not covered in the mainstream media.

Telesur was not promoted as being counter-hegemonic in the sense of being anti-American or anti-Bush. But even before it had time to bed down, its very existence provoked strong reactions from Republican Congressmen in the United States. Soon after its launch, Connie Mack, a pugnacious Florida Republican, described Chávez as an 'enemy of freedom' who wanted to use Telesur to 'poison the mind of people longing to be free', while Richard Lugar, the chair of the US Senate's foreign relations committee, said it was a vehicle to spread Chávez's authoritarian message around Latin America.

Telesur's formal association with Al-Jazeera (Arabic) announced in January 2006 (mostly in the exchange of pictures, training, resources and technological support) was part of the reason for the opposition from the Republican right. A close relationship with AJA, which they view as having an anti-American agenda, confirmed their suspicions of a channel funded by another of their bugbears, Hugo Chávez. But for Telesur's president, Andrés Izarra, AJA was an inspirational model for Telesur because of 'its different point of view, different voice, its closeness to the people, and its closer view of the Arab world with all its diversity and contradictions'.[97]

Information hegemony

President Chávez's victory in the elections of December 2006 represented a new departure in his policies towards the state and the media. Prior to then, the media environment (into which Telesur was born) was one in

[96] The best expression of this can be found in Florencia Copley, 'Telesur is Constructing Another View', <venezuela.analysis.com>, 14 Dec. 2005. Aram Aharonian, Telesur's general director, talks of reversing the information flow from South to North in a manner recommended by the 1980 MacBride UNESCO report. See his article at <www.telesurtv.net/v3/secciones/notasdeopinion>.

[97] Author interview, 30 Oct. 2006. A comparison with AJA is not an idle one. Both are targeted by the Republican right, both are funded by oil money, both have had senior staff working in mainstream media before changing allegiance, both are accused of having a political agenda, and both have had correspondents arrested on charges of close links with armed groups. However, there are important differences, for which see Cañizález and Lugo, 'Telesur'.

which journalistic standards of balance, impartiality and independence had been eclipsed by partisan coverage,[98] but one still marked by a considerable degree of pluralism of media outlets. This changed on 28 December when Chávez announced he would not be renewing the broadcasting licence of RCTV when it expired in May 2007. RCTV's terrestrial frequency was to be given to a new national public service television, eventually called TVes, although RCTV would be allowed to broadcast as a cable channel. It was the first time Chávez had made such a move. He justified it by reminding the world of the station's support for the April 2002 coup. Government officials denounced the 'untouchable dictatorship of a few oligarchic families over large television and radio media'.

Izarra, who used to work at RCTV, played a very public role in arguing the case for the decision. He was widely quoted as saying that at the time of the coup RCTV had broadcast 64 days of propaganda exclusively against the government. Izarra was also clearly taking on an important task in the overall direction of the state's policy towards the media. In January 2007, Chávez announced several measures, including the nationalisation of the telecommunications and electricity industries, which were widely seen as deepening the socialist revolution. As part of this radicalization, Izarra for his part confirmed a 'new strategic plan' for the media, which included the non-renewal of RCTV's licence and the purchase of a Venezuelan television frequency (previously owned by Caracas Metropolitan Television) for Telesur, which would allow it to have a much wider presence within Venezuela.[99] In the interview, Izarra spelt out that the aim was to 'construct a communications and information hegemony that will allow an ideological and cultural battle to promote socialism'.

Such statements added substance to the fears of Chávez's critics that he was going down the route of a more totalitarian media model. The Inter-American Press Association, which tends to represent the views of Latin America's media proprietors, was probably the most vociferous in denouncing the partial closure of RCTV and Chávez's control of the media. It claimed the government was spending no less than US$800m in 2007 on its various state channels including Telesur, TVes and 3,000 radio

---

[98] The Venezuelan press watchdog, Observatorio, has tracked the strong or moderate bias of the media, particularly in the coverage of elections. For example, in the run-up to the Dec. 2006 elections, it concluded that RCTV was biased in favour of the opposition candidate but the domestic state channel VTV was worse in favour of Chávez. A similar conclusion was reached by the European Union's team monitoring the elections. Unfortunately Telesur's coverage was not included in either report.
[99] 'TV President Outlines Venezuelan Government's Media Strategy', *El Nacional* website, <http://www.el-nacional.com/> (8 Jan. 2007), tr. BBC Monitoring.

stations.[100] Whatever the exact figure, the large sums of money did not prevent Chávez from narrowly losing another referendum in December 2007, which if successful, would have allowed him to centralize power, stay in office for life and accelerate his path towards 21st-century socialism. In response to his defeat, on 4 January 2008 Chávez announced wide-ranging changes to his cabinet, including the appointment of Izarra to his old position of information minister. Part of Izarra's brief was to review the role of VTV and TVes, which, as Chávez himself said, 'hardly anyone watches', and to establish a network of alternative media to boost the 'communication capacity' of the revolution.[101]

In such a polarised media climate inside Venezuela, it would have been extraordinary if Telesur had followed a neutral editorial position. As already mentioned, *prima facie* its advertisements, documentaries and round-table discussions plus Izarra's background suggested a strong left-wing and pro-Chávez orientation. However, Izarra continued to insist in interviews that Telesur was not TeleChávez. He told the EFE news agency in May 2007 that Telesur 'stick[s] to the most basic journalistic principles of thoroughness, balance, pluralism and relying on multiple sources'.[102] So does Telesur have an obvious bias? What is its editorial distinctiveness or profile?

---

[100] IAPA report on Venezuela at its 63rd General Assembly, available at
<http://mercury.websitewelcome.com/~sipiapa/informe.php?id=24&idioma=us>
[101] 'Chávez Announces Major Cabinet Reshuffle', <*Venezuelanalysis.com*> (4 Jan. 2008).
[102] EFE newsagency, 'Venezuela-Based TV Network Telesur Seeks Foothold in Spain' (8 May 2007).

5 Telesur or Telechávez?

It is not within the scope of this study to enter into the long and important debate about the differences between objectivity, balance, neutrality and impartiality. However, it seems useful to repeat apply the BBC guidelines on impartiality already mentioned in the introduction: it aims

> *to provide a properly balanced service consisting of a wide range of subject matter and views broadcast over an appropriate time scale,* [and] *to reflect a wide range of opinion and explore a range and conflict of views so that no significant strand of thought is knowingly unreflected or under represented.*[103]

With this in mind, one way to test whether Telesur is clearly aspiring to be impartial and avoid bias is to assess the following four hypotheses through content analysis of its news programmes over several days:

(1) Telesur in general selects information favourable to a pro-Chávez or leftist agenda (and in particular in favour of the Bolivian and Cuban governments, and against President Bush).

(2) In its coverage of elections in the Americas, Telesur favours pro-Chávez, anti-Bush or left-wing candidates.

(3) Telesur in its coverage of Venezuela has a pro-Chávez bias.

(4) Telesur uses a preponderance of left-wing analysts and commentators.

---

[103] The BBC editorial guidelines are available online at
<http://www.bbc.co.uk/guidelines/editorialguidelines>.
Historically the BBC has aimed to follow the concept of 'due impartiality' when covering news, although Peter Horrocks, the current head of BBC Television News, prefers the concept of 'radical impartiality' which includes 'the need to hear the widest range of views'. See his lecture given at Oxford University on 28 Nov. 2006 reproduced at <reutersinstitute.politics.ox.ac.uk/news/opinion/tv_news.htm>.

Testing hypothesis (1)

This hypothesis was tested by assessing what CNN and Telesur regarded as newsworthy over a number of nights. The programmes chosen for analysis were Telesur's and CNN en español's flagship evening news programmes at 2000 Caracas-time (0000 GMT) on three nights in November 2006 (5th, 7th and 8th). They were selected in part because they included coverage of the presidential elections in Nicaragua (on 5 November) and the mid-term Congressional elections in the USA (on 7 November). The following conclusions can be drawn:[104]

(i) Neither channel is falsifying news, but choosing items to include according to different news criteria.

(ii) CNN and Telesur have at times very different news priorities, and a different sense of what is newsworthy. CNN put more emphasis on the coverage of US elections at a time when Telesur was concentrating much more on the Nicaraguan elections and other stories in Latin America. Telesur provided a wider breadth of coverage of the Nicaraguan election, which included the political, social and economic context. CNN did not offer the same breadth of regional stories that Telesur provided, but provided considerably more information on events in the USA.

(iii) At times they covered similar themes, and there was a large degree of overlap of similar material and angles to the stories. However, there is evidence to suggest that Telesur favours information that is pro-Cuba and either openly or by implication critical of the Bush administration. In contrast, in the newscasts studied, CNN ran no material that could be seen to be pro-Cuba and little that was critical of the Bush administration's foreign policy towards Iraq or Cuba.

So an analysis of what stories Telesur decides to cover and how it covers them would seem to confirm hypothesis (1). What other evidence is there to support this view? An examination of BBC Monitoring's summaries of Telesur's main news bulletin at 0000 GMT[105] (on the 20 weekdays between 30 October and 24 November 2006) suggests very little criticism of Cuba, nor of two of Telesur's other sponsor governments, Venezuela and Bolivia.[106]

---

[104] For a fuller discussion of the programmes on which the conclusions are based, see Painter, 'Boom', ch 4.
[105] BBC Monitoring provide itemised and detailed summaries on weekdays of Telesur's output at 0000 GMT. This includes summaries of all the items of the programme, including a brief résumé of the content, time allocation, details of the source of the footage, the names of correspondents and the main participants in each item.
[106] A fuller picture would be achieved by analysing Telesur's coverage of Argentina, another sponsor government of the station. However, in the period in question, there was little coverage of Argentina. Also Argentina did not form part of the 'axis of good' (Venezuela, Bolivia and Cuba) which Chávez was championing at the time.

There were several items criticising the US blockade of Cuba, usually illustrated by interviews with Cuban officials, but none criticising any aspect of Cuba. On Bolivia, virtually all of the stories were mainly from the point of the view of the government of President Evo Morales, using predominantly pictures of the president, his ministers or his supporters. On Venezuela, there were several items stressing a government point of view on an issue or mentioning the achievements of President Chávez. There was one item showing the main opposition candidate, Manuel Rosales, but the overwhelming weight of the coverage included pictures of Hugo Chávez, government ministers or other supporters.

Such an examination of programme summaries should not of course be considered infallible, but it does corroborate a preliminary view that Telesur is not showing its editorial independence from three of the main governments that fund or sponsor it by subjecting them to any serious critical coverage. On the contrary, it broadcasts plenty of material which puts them in a good light.

Testing hypothesis (2)

The coverage of the Nicaraguan presidential elections on Sunday 5 November was chosen to test hypothesis (2). The fact that Daniel Ortega, candidate for the left-wing Sandinistas and a political ally of President Chávez, was running against two pro-US candidates makes it a good choice to test bias.

A quantitative and qualitative analysis of Telesur's coverage on the night of 5 November (starting at 0000 GMT) does suggest that all four candidates were treated in an even-handed manner.[107] Daniel Ortega was criticised by one opponent for only being interested in power, a view which is echoed by some of his former supporters.[108] There was also mention of his political transformation, most noticeably symbolised by his alliance with a former right-wing contra rebel as a running mate and his reconciliation with the Catholic Church. Given President Chávez's open support for Mr Ortega, it would not have been unreasonable to have predicted an overwhelming bias in favour of his candidate. But this was clearly not the case.

---

[107] Painter, 'Boom', tables 4.3 and 4.4.
[108] The international coverage, including by British newspapers with a left-liberal profile like the *Guardian* and *Observer*, was far more critical of Ortega, in particular for his pact in 2001 with the corrupt former Nicaraguan president, Arnoldo Aleman, which resulted in his gaining immunity from prosecution for the alleged sexual abuse of his stepdaughter.

This examination of Telesur's coverage of the Nicaraguan elections would therefore suggest some degree of balance. Moreover, an examination of BBC Monitoring's programme summaries of Telesur's *Noticias* programme on weekdays (at 0000 GMT) in the three weeks before the elections would suggest at least a degree of pluralism in the coverage. The reports on Nicaragua included video clips of all the candidates, the closing rallies of Ortega and two other candidates, and criticism of Venezuela's oil supplies to Sandinista-controlled local governments. The Nicaraguan government did not at the time of the coverage of the elections make any financial or other contribution to Telesur, so it could be argued there was more room for editorial independence. But there is initial evidence to suggest that the channel exhibits some pluralism in its coverage of non-sponsoring countries, but is largely uncritical of those with a stake in it.

Testing hypothesis (3)

Hypothesis (3) was tested by analysing the coverage of Venezuela's presidential elections held on 3 December 2006, and in particular the 0000 GMT or 0100 GMT edition of *Telesur Noticias* on four consecutive nights (2, 3, 4 and 5 December). Some comparisons were made both with CNN en español's coverage on the same nights and with the coverage of some of the mainstream Western media.

In the months running up to the elections, there were fears from the *chavistas* that the opposition parties would boycott the elections in the same way that they had decided at a late stage not to take part in the National Assembly elections of December 2005 (and thereby deny them legitimacy). In the event, most of the opposition united around the candidature of Manuel Rosales, the governor of the western state of Zulia. Most opinion polls gave Chávez a 20-point lead over Rosales. Despite the polls, some of the opposition feared that Chávez would win by fraud and mistrusted the independence of the government-dominated electoral authority, the CNE. In particular, there were concerns expressed by the opposition over the fingerprint machines (used in conjunction with the electronic voting).[109]

The government dismissed the allegations of possible fraud. They said robust technological and administrative procedures were in place to prevent

---

[109] The grounds for their fears was the so-called Tascon list, which had identified people who added their signatures to a call for the 2004 referendum and was reported to have led to some being barred from government jobs and access to some public services.

software manipulation or other security failures.[110] They also pointed to the fact that the elections were one of the most observed anywhere in the world, with a huge presence of international observers including those from the OAS, the Carter Center and the European Union. In addition, observers from the parties taking part in the elections were entitled to observe the 33,000 polling stations throughout the country.

The issue of possible fraud dominated the national coverage of the elections. Many privately owned media outlets focused on the possibility of fraud and what form it might take, whereas the pro-government media carried reports of what they said was evidence of the opposition planning for post-electoral violence and/or demonstrations. This allegedly included plans for a coup and lists of people plotting to assassinate the president, including opposition figures and the Bush administration. Considerable attention was paid to the allegations that the Rosales camp had already prepared campaign leaflets, banners and T-shirts for a massive campaign soon after the elections to denounce fraud.

The international media did not give as much coverage to the accusations and counter-accusations. Rather, their focus was on the overwhelming support for Chávez from the poorer sectors of society as a result of his social programmes, and in particular the so-called Misiones. These consist of free health care, popular education and subsidised supermarkets, all of which the large oil revenues had helped to fund. Even the *Financial Times* and *The Economist*, which are not known for their pro-Chávez sentiments, stressed the wide appeal of the Misiones. But they also included criticisms of poor crime figures, ongoing corruption and increasing authoritarianism, all of which were also mentioned by correspondents from other Western media less opposed to Chávez.[111] Manuel Rosales was not given much chance of success. In the event, Chávez won an overwhelming majority with 62.9 per cent of the vote while Rosales won just under 40 per cent. Soon after the vote, Rosales accepted that it was free of fraud.

Telesur's programme on 2 December (0000 GMT) showed token balance by offering profiles of roughly equal length of both candidates and by running

---

[110] A good summary of this can be found in the briefing document distributed prior to the elections by the London-based, pro-Chávez Venezuela Information Centre, 'Venezuela: Democracy and Social Progress', available at
<http://www.vicuk.org/index.php?option=com_content&task=view&id=156&Itemid=30>
[111] 'The Chávez Machine Rolls on', *The Economist* (30 Nov. 2006). Richard Lapper, 'Petro-Populism: A Third Term Beckons for Venezuela's Firebrand President', *Financial Times* (1 Dec. 2006). Rory Carroll, 'Charisma and Petro-Dollars Mean the Show Will Go On for Chávez', *Guardian* (2 Dec. 2006). Simon Romero, 'Crime is Top Concern for Venezuela Voters', *International Herald Tribune* (2 Dec. 2006). Nathalie Malinarich, 'Venezuela: A Nation Divided', BBC News website (27 Nov. 2006), <http://news.bbc.co.uk/1/hi/world/americas/6179612.stm>

interviews (again of roughly equal length) with representatives of both of their campaign teams. But content analysis shows the essentially partisan nature of the coverage.[112] There were few, if any, negative aspects mentioned in the profile of Chávez compared to the profile of Rosales. The interviews with the representatives of the campaign teams were conducted very differently in terms of the questions asked and the tone of the interviews. Virtually no criticism of Chávez was included in the coverage, even though any one of the problems mentioned above could have been covered (housing shortages, rising violent crime, corruption and authoritarian elements to his style of government). The profile of Rosales could have included some positive comments such as his success in making the opposition more unified.[113]

Telesur's programme on the night of 3 December (0000 GMT) in many ways showed its true colours. The channel clearly responded to a political, and not a journalistic, imperative. Its editors on the night took the highly controversial decision to 'jump the gun' and broadcast preliminary unofficial results based on exit polls, despite a call from the CNE, backed up by the OAS, insisting all media should wait until the official results were given. The programme at 0000 GMT (broadcast just as the polls were closing) opened with the news in the mouth of the presenter that the exit polls gave Chávez a lead over Rosales of 67–33 per cent. This was illustrated with a graphic. The presenter announced that the Venezuelan people had given another six years to the incumbent president, Hugo Chávez. The same message was repeated twice more in the first section of the programme, first by the station's reporter reporting live from the CNE headquarters in Caracas, and then again by the presenter. Each time the phrase was used that the next president of Venezuela would be Hugo Chávez. In short, about 6 minutes of the first 11 minutes of the programme was designed to announce and then reinforce the message that Chávez had won.

The calls not to publish exit polls had been given considerable publicity. The night before, CNN en español headlined the words of the OAS secretary general, José Miguel Inzulza, who had reminded media and parties alike not to disseminate unofficial results as they could 'provoke undesired

---

[112] For a fuller discussion see Painter, 'Boom', pp. 41–6.
[113] In the profiles of the two candidates on the BBC News website, for example, the one on Chávez includes the view of the opposition that he is autocratic, and that despite the oil wealth, there is chronic poverty and widespread unemployment <http://news.bbc.co.uk/1/hi/world/americas/3517106.stm>. The profile of Rosales includes the view that he has been able to 'energise a demoralised and divided opposition', and the accusation of his involvement in the April 2002 coup <http://news.bbc.co.uk/2/hi/americas/6180358.stm>.

reactions'. Ironically, Telesur itself had broadcast on the same night a similar message from the OAS representative at the elections, Juan Fischer. In the week before, the OAS observer mission had met representatives of the media precisely to agree that no one should provide any results until the first bulletin of the CNE.

So why did Telesur take the decision it did? Both prior to and after the elections, Izarra maintained that the station was an international one, and therefore not bound by the same rules as a domestic station. In a statement issued on Telesur's website soon after the elections, Telesur stressed this point and added that its mission was to 'offer balanced and truthful information about events which the large news channels omit or distort'. It added that various agencies opted to publish the exit polls, and others did not, and that it belonged to the former group.

The argument that it was an international channel and not bound by the rules is insubstantial. The BBC Global News Division was advised by the CNE that it had to follow the rules governing domestic media as it can be seen by viewers within Venezuela, and so was regarded as a domestic broadcaster. Likewise, at the time Telesur could be seen via VTV in Venezuela. Both the BBC and CNN did not broadcast the exit polls, but waited for the first bulletin giving the official results (which came shortly afterwards at 0110 GMT (2110 Venezuela time). Izarra said that Reuters and 'Argentina and Spain' had reported the results internationally.[114] But the Reuters cable came with a clear disclaimer at the top saying it was illegal to publish it within Venezuela.

Telesur's decision to broadcast the exit polls was certainly known widely within Venezuela. Globovision in its live coverage from 0030 GMT (2030 Venezuela time) was already broadcasting live statements by incandescent opposition representatives saying the figures were absolutely false and denouncing Telesur's action as a serious abuse of the electoral rules. They said all the other media had respected the agreement to wait for the official results and that Telesur was not exempt as it was 80 per cent owned by the Venezuelan government. Telesur itself ran several minutes of a live impromptu press conference given at 0045 GMT by Willian Lara, the communications minister, within its programme. Lara was bombarded with questions from a mass of journalists about Telesur's decision, which he declined to answer, saying he would comment on the elections results once they were official. International viewers must have wondered what all the fuss was about, but

[114] Interview with Izarra, 'TV President Outlines Venezuelan Government's Media Strategy', *El Nacional* website, <http://el-nacional.com> 8 Jan. 2007, tr. BBC Monitoring>.

within Venezuela it was obvious that Telesur's action and the figures it was broadcasting were widely known.

So what was the real reason behind Telesur's decision to broadcast the exit polls? The most likely explanation is to be found within the tense pre- and post-electoral climate and rumours of what the opposition would do in the event of a Chávez victory. Telesur directors probably calculated that some of the opposition was going to cry fraud and start anti-Chávez mobilisations if it thought it was losing. So broadcasting exit polls showing Chávez with a big majority would help to pre-empt such an attempt. Some evidence for this explanation is to be found in an article published by *El Nacional*, in which sources consulted by the paper said Izarra had interpreted a comment by a leading member of the Rosales campaign Teodoro Petkoff as the key for the opposition to take to the streets and protest alleged fraud. '[Izarra] acted on his own', the paper said quoting the sources, 'as he sought to neutralise any opposition attempt to cause uncertainty'.[115]

Whatever the reason, Telesur clearly took an editorial decision, not shared by most international media, to report information which was both highly controversial and clearly intended to have a political impact in Venezuela in favour of the Chávez government. In a sense, Telesur had viewed the issue through the prism of a state broadcaster responding to political and not journalistic considerations. Speculation was rife after the elections that the government had been so embarrassed by Telesur's decision that Willian Lara would have to resign. In fact, Lara was reconfirmed as Information Minister in the cabinet reshuffle in early 2007, but an investigation was set in motion by the CNE with the possibility of Telesur receiving penalties or fines. In the months that followed, there was no information about Telesur being fined.

On the night of 4/5 December, more than 90 per cent of the votes had been counted and official results were giving Chávez around 62 per cent of the vote compared to about 37 per cent for Rosales. At 0100 GMT CNN and Telesur both led with the news of Chávez's victory and allocated a good part of their respective programmes to reactions and analysis. Telesur decided to include the congratulations for Chávez from around Latin America, including President Evo Morales of Bolivia, two from Colombia (the government and a Liberal Party senator), President Kirchner of Argentina, president-elect Rafael Correa of Ecuador (and the Spanish foreign minister). In contrast, CNN just ran that of the US government.

---

[115] 'Willian Lara Dismissed from the Communications Industry', *El Nacional* website, 5 Dec. 2006, tr. BBC Monitoring.

Telesur had no analysis of what the results meant either for Chávez or the opposition whereas CNN ran a clip of an analyst saying Chávez needed to be more tolerant in the future, and a commentary in the words of one of their reporters saying that, despite their defeat, the opposition felt optimistic about their new-found unity. Finally, the analyst used by Telesur was the first secretary of the Communist Party of Uruguay (an observer of the elections) who interpreted the elections results in Venezuela (and Ecuador) as two major blows for US imperialism.

In short, the Telesur programme left the viewer with the impression of a Chávez victory celebrated across Latin America, but representing a defeat for the Bush administration. It offered no mention or analysis of where the elections left the opposition.

By the following night, Venezuela had dropped out of the headlines of CNN's programme, whereas it led Telesur's programme. The latter's coverage lasted more than six minutes, and included Chávez's press conference where he stressed that Venezuela would travel further down the road towards 21st-century socialism, and that he was willing to hold dialogue with the United States (although he saw difficulties). The sequence also included clips of Chávez supporters; congratulations from Fidel Castro and Cubans (part of Castro's letter read out by the presenter plus video footage), President Ahmadinejad of Iran (archive video) and three other leaders of Libya, Chile and Italy (read out by presenter); and Rosales's press conference in which he accepted the results of the elections as clean. CNN on the other hand only included only a short piece of 1.20 minutes as fourth item in their programme, which included clips of Chávez's press conference mentioning the possibility of dialogue with the USA, and one of the presenters reading out the letter of congratulation from Fidel Castro.

Telesur clearly thought that the Chávez victory was still the top Latin American story of the day in contrast to CNN. Moreover, the emphasis of its coverage was again on the positive reactions from around the world. Rosales was included but only in so far his statements lent credence to Chávez's victory.

Testing hypothesis (4)

One final way of testing bias is to review the political profile of the analysts and commentators used in a station's coverage. This gives insights into the interpretation of events rather than the recounting of events. If only one or a restricted number of viewpoints are being given air, then obviously it is not unnatural to conclude that a station, either consciously or not, is promoting a particular interpretation of what is going on. It is also important to 'label' analysts correctly so as to give viewers an idea of what sort of opinions or understanding of events the interviewees are likely to be offering. If editors are interested in avoiding bias, then the norm is to make it clear when contributors are associated with a particular viewpoint.

A review of the six analysts used by Telesur over the course of the four nights shows that they all gave a pro-Chávez interpretation of what they were being asked to analyse.[116] There was no analysis from a more independent standpoint. Moreover, some of the on-screen labelling was disingenuous. Of the analysts used, one was described as a university teacher but is a known government supporter (Tibisay Hung), another was described as a lawyer and author but has written a book very critical of US operations in Venezuela (Eva Golinger), another was presented as an international lawyer but is a left-wing academic who has his own pro-Chávez radio programme on state radio (Vladimir Acosta), and another was presented as a senator from Colombia's Liberal Party but it was not mentioned she is on the left-wing of the Liberal Party and is very critical of US actions in her country (Piedad Cordoba). All of these analysts are legitimate interviewees, but it is not unreasonable to ask for more description of their background, at least in the words of the presenter. When such descriptions are not forthcoming, the viewer could legitimately complain that the analysts are being presented as offering more independent or objective analysis than knowledge of their background would suggest.

Conclusions

So what can be concluded from the analysis of Telesur's coverage?
(1) Telesur is not falsifying the news, but choosing news stories according to different editorial criteria to those of CNN for example.
(2) There is strong evidence to suggest that Telesur selects information that puts its sponsoring governments in a favourable light, in particular Cuba and Bolivia, and puts President Bush in a bad light.
(3) There is some evidence to suggest that Telesur is more pluralistic in its coverage of countries who are not sponsoring the channel, but this would have to be corroborated by more content analysis of countries like Colombia, Mexico and Peru whose governments are not supporters of President Chávez.

[116] For a fuller discussion, see Painter, 'Boom', 49–50.

(4) There is overwhelming evidence to suggest that the coverage of Venezuela is strongly partisan in favour of President Chávez. This was plainly the case in its coverage of the Venezuelan elections of December 2006: the depiction of the two candidates and their respective electoral programmes or achievements was not even-handed. After the elections, there was a prolonged emphasis on Chávez's victory and the international reaction to it (which was all favourable). The tone of the coverage was often celebratory. In the choice of analysts to be interviewed, there was a strong if not total propensity to offer a pro-Chávez, anti-Bush perspective. And finally, in making the decision to broadcast exit polls on the night of the elections, the station responded to a perceived political response in favour of the government. For a time that night, its decision became the news of the moment. It behaved more like a state television channel at the service of a government rather than a public service international broadcaster.

Conclusion

Telesur's essential aim is political. It forms one plank of President Chávez' strategy to counter the perceived hegemony of the United States. His strategy is not dissimilar to the efforts of President Putin in Russia and President Ahmadinejad in Iran to combine oil or gas revenue with forceful anti-US rhetoric and policies. It is no coincidence that all three have invested heavily in 24/7 news channels to counter what they see as the cultural and news imperialism of the West, and the United States in particular.

It can be said that it is offering a new voice and perspective in a crowded and uniform market.[117] A viewer can see more coverage of some countries, issues and voices from Latin America than would be available on most national television stations where the vast majority of Latin Americans receive their news about the world. It shows much less propensity to include perspectives from Washington than CNN for example, and much more about under-reported countries like Haiti and particularly countries whose governments are pro-Chávez like President Evo Morales of Bolivia. It certainly includes more voices from left-wing rebels, parties or social movements. All this is not presented in the crude style of old-fashioned propaganda. This has historically been characterised by long-winded speeches from political leaders, extreme deference to those leaders, an emphasis on government achievements, negative news being kept to a minimum, few critical voices of the government, extensive coverage of visiting heads of state and an abundance of ordinary people being portrayed as benefiting from the state.[118]

---

[117] For a fuller discussion of the characteristics of Telesur, ibid., ch. 6.
[118] This was the template, for example, of Mexico's Televisa before 1990, and remains that of CCTV in China, Radio Havana in Cuba and the state Venezuelan station VTV. At times Telesur in its coverage of Venezuela begins to lapse into this style, but it is usually sufficiently distinct in its treatment of stories not to be labelled as old-style propaganda.

Like most of the new wave of channels, Telesur's style and programmes formats are essentially copied from traditional Western channels. The trappings are adopted, but not the journalistic values. Telesur is more in the Latin American tradition of state-funded channels acting as official megaphones than in the Western European tradition of public service channels aiming to offer impartiality, pluralism of view or a watchdog role holding sponsoring governments and powerful actors to account. Although it shows some pluralism in covering countries where governments are not sponsoring the channel, there is virtually no criticism of sponsoring governments and particularly of President Chávez.

Telesur is counter-hegemonic in virtually all of the senses discussed in this study. Like most of the new 24/7 news channels, it aims to take on the domination of Western media like CNN and the BBC and offer different content and a different perspective. It also aims to present 'news from the south', which means in Telesur's case not just more news from Latin America but more voices that do not normally get on the air. It is also counter-hegemonic in the narrow sense of being anti-Western governments, and specifically anti-Bush.

However, it is far from clear if Telesur is counter-hegemonic in the sense of reversing the flow of information from the West to the rest, or even of effectively taking on the domination of CNN in the Latin American market. It is officially available in 17 countries and in 2–3 million cable or satellite homes. Its terrestrial distribution is largely restricted to state channels in countries where the government is sponsoring the station. Reliable market figures are hard to come by, but one recent estimate suggested that it had an audience, in the best of cases, of less than 500,000 people.[119] Latin Americans' historical mistrust of state channels is just one reason why Telesur will find it difficult to be more than a niche channel broadcasting to left-wing sympathisers.

AJE is far more balanced in its treatment of news than Telesur and other state-funded channels like Russia Today and Press TV. In the first year of its existence, for the most part, in its news programmes AJE seemed to stay on the side of non-partisan coverage and did not act as an unchallenged spokesperson for any government, political grouping or oppressed minority from the south. Giving more coverage to such Southern voices seemed to stay on the right side of correcting imbalance rather than slipping into the espousal of a cause. To use its own phrase, the 'setting of the news agenda' lay much more in its selection of news stories than in its biased treatment

---

[119] Cañizález and Lugo, 'Telesur'. In 2002, CNN en español had a measured audience of 12 million in Latin America, and it has increased since then.

of them. Moreover, it was not 'counter-hegemonic' in the sense of being anti-Western governments, although it was in the sense of offering something different to the main Western media.

It is beyond the scope of this report to assess whether AJE also counters the trend often decried in 24/7 news channels of offering 'infotainment' and superficiality in place of depth and understanding. But it does seem to be the case from an impressionistic examination that AJE does try to give more context and analysis to many stories from developing countries, partly because it has more time in its news programmes at its disposal.[120] Two respected commentators have commended AJE for its analysis and depth of coverage of Lebanon and Iran respectively.[121]

However, at the time of writing, AJE was going through turbulent times. In the early months of 2008 a number of serious problems affecting the channel came out in the open, which some commentators saw as threatening the very survival of the channel. These included low staff morale, rows over salary differentials between AJE and AJA staff, resignations by some high-profile presenters and managers, compensation claims for unfair dismissal, low viewing figures and lack of sufficient funds for marketing and promotion.[122] In the editorial sphere, a potentially very damaging tension had surfaced again which threatened both the future of the channel and the primacy of its 'Southern perspective'. Press reports suggested that there was a battle going on over the degree to which news at AJE should be given an 'Islamic slant'.[123] This in turn reflected a wider conflict within the Al-Jazeera organisation between the mainly Western directors of AJE and the executives of the wider Al-Jazeera network. There was a clear possibility that more political pressure would be brought to bear on AJE to bring it more into line with AJA's editorial priorities.

Fuel was added to the fire by comments from AJE's US presenter David Marash at the time of his resignation in March. He complained of an increased level of editorial control exercised by AJE's headquarters in Doha, and of what he saw as an anti-American bias in the AJE's coverage.[124]

---

[120] The downside is that many of its reports seem more like features than hard news stories, which lays it open to the criticism of being too worthy and over-educational, like a pro-poor third world feature service.
[121] Pintak, 'Will Al-Jazeera English Find its Groove?', and Peter Preston, 'BBC is Trying to Do Too Much', *Observer* (21 Oct. 2007).
[122] See for example, James Robinson, 'New Boss is Determined to Keep the Faith at Al-Jazeera', *Observer* (8 June 2008), and Jane England, 'Al-Jazeera English Tackles Staff Disquiet', *Financial Times* (27 May 2008). Author interviews with AJE staff confirm these press reports.
[123] Holmwood, 'Al-Jazeera English in "Staffing Crisis"', and Dan Sabbagh, 'Us-and-Them Syndrome Eats Away at Al-Jazeera English', <http://www.timesonline.co.uk> (1 Feb. 2008).
[124] Brian Stelter, 'American Anchor Quits Al Jazeera English Channel', *New York Times* (28 March 2009), and Brent Cunningham, 'Dave Marash: Why I Quit', *Columbia Journalism Review* (4 April 2008).

Marash later regretted that he had used the term 'anti-American', but clarified his criticisms saying that 'the people in the network's Doha headquarters (many of whom are British) have a view of America that is really shallow and stereotyped'.[125]

AA new managing director, Tony Burman, a former head of CBC news, was appointed in May. He said his main priorities were to increase in-depth journalism and to crack the US and Canadian market,[126] but he was clearly on a mission to save the channel. He flatly denied that there interesting to note that the director-general of Al-Jazeera Networks, Wadah Khanfar, stressed that Burman's appointment was to enrich AJE's core mission, which included its dedication to giving 'a voice to the voiceless and ensuring that the human story is at the centre of the news agenda'.

Despite all its problems and staff changes, AJE's editorial perspective, if maintained intact, had the potential at least of remaining a key element of its possible long-term success. AJE's supporters pointed out that CNN took ten years to make a breakthrough after its launch in 1980. AJE's combination of this distinctive editorial perspective, a secure and heavily endowed financial base and pluralistic journalistic values could still in theory be a recipe for a long-term presence in a crowded market.

It is too early to tell if AJE will have such a presence, and indeed have an impact on reversing traditional information flows from the north to the south. In early 2008 AJE managers claimed the channel was available in 110 million homes in 60 countries around the world, but global or regional figures were not available for actual viewership. It had of course a long way to catch up with BBC World's 2008 global audience of 78 million a week or with CNNI's audience, which is thought to be over 100 million.

In theory at least, targeting a more general audience than CNNI and BBCW could give AJE a long-term edge over its rivals. CNNI aims at business classes with an interest in world affairs, whilst BBCW aims for 'influencers and news followers', but still in the main a political and economic elite.[127] Broadcasting more stories from the developing world is bound to increase AJE's attractiveness to a large chunk of its target audience in English-speaking

---

[125] Erin Sullivan, 'Doha Calling: Al Jazeera English Could Change the Way You See the World – If You Ever Get to Watch It', *Baltimore City Paper* (7 May 2008), available at <http://www.citypaper.com/columns/story.asp?id=15691>.
[126] 'Al-Jazeera TV is the Voice of the Voice-less', Qatar newspaper *Al-Sharq* (17 May 2008), tr. BBC Monitoring.
[127] It is an interesting question as to what extent AJE's editorial perspective is driven by its target audience. It is probably fair to assume that there is a happy coincidence of interests between AJE's main target audiences and its different editorial perspective.

(Muslim) parts of the world in South and South-East Asia, Africa and the Middle East.[128] After all, about 80 per cent of the world's Muslims do not speak Arabic. However, like most international channels, AJE was finding it very difficult to have a presence in the US cable and satellite market: it was restricted to three small distributors, its internet site and YouTube. But its absence from the Chinese and Indian markets was equally disappointing for a channel taking pride in offering a Southern perspective.

One final important issue to consider is whether the boom in channels like Telesur and Al-Jazeera English is shifting the media landscape further down the path towards biased TV and further away from the notion that there can be an unbiased news channel. Telesur would fall into the category, like Russia Today, CCTV-9 and Press TV, of those channels with a strong, conscious, political agenda. They can be seen as part of a more general trend observed in different parts of the world of a proliferation of 'news with views'. The growth in new 24/7 channels shares some characteristics with the growth in news websites which makes it more possible for a news consumer to choose a source of information which confirms his or her particular point of view. Fox News is the classic example of this, but there are plenty of others. Such a trend is welcome in that it adds to the plurality of voices, enhances choice and perspective, and in many cases can correct an information imbalance. But the casualty of 'agenda-driven news' is surely going to be the attempt to be fair, impartial and accurate. There is also considerable evidence from the US that the proliferation of channels with an agenda does not add to consumers' understanding of the news, particularly when media outlets often disguise their bias with public espousals of balance.[129]

Al-Jazeera English falls into a different category. Like CNN and the BBC, it follows journalistic values such as balance and plurality of opinion.

---

[128] Official figures for the geographical breakdown in audiences are not available, but AJE executives say they are 'doing well' in Africa, the Middle East and South-East Asia. One report suggested that, of the 110 million homes where AJE is available, 22 million were in Asia. See Liz Gooch, 'Courage Under Fire Attacked by the US and Mauled in the Mideast, Al-Jazeera Soldiered on', *South China Morning Post* (16 May 2008).

[129] Fox News runs the slogan 'we report, you decide', which implies a degree of impartiality. But the channel has been widely found to have a pro-Republican bias, and to be much more likely to be watched by Republican voters. Studies in the US have shown that the boom in partisan news has had a negative impact on the understanding or interpretation of news. For example, in one survey, four-fifths of Fox viewers believed one of the following: Iraq was directly involved in September 11; world opinion favoured the Iraq war; and weapons of mass destruction had already been discovered. Less than a quarter of the listeners and viewers of National Public Radio or PBS made the same mistake. Quoted by Richard Lambert in his Wincott lecture, Oct. 2006, available at
<http://www.ft.com/cms/s/2/f345f3fe-6901-11db-b4c2-0000779e2340.html>.

Editors at CNN and BBCW do not consciously follow any agenda other than a journalistic one, but many observers would of course argue that they do unconsciously represent a cultural bias in the stories they choose to report and in the perspective they offer on those stories. Expressed crudely, this unconscious 'attitudinal' set of values can mean in practice an abundance of stories about terrorism affecting Western capitals but not much about the four million people killed in the Democratic Republic of Congo or the millions affected by malaria around the world. At its worst, it can mean a lack of scrutiny of Western governments in their justification for, and their conduct in, the war in Iraq.

In contrast, AJE is consciously following a weak political agenda by covering far more news from 'the south'. There are pitfalls to such an approach. Ignoring or down-playing events in the West can mean a viewer will miss out on what actually drives a large part of international relations. Covering under-reported parts of the world in great depth may be a very worthy policy, but it may sound like an Oxfam or UN channel and put off viewers if the journalism does not remain sharp-edged. Putting more 'voices of oppressed south' on air can slide into too uncritical a view of their actions or proposed solutions to their suffering, or it may focus too much on a 'suffering south' at the expense of an 'assertive south'.

The tension between AJE's different perspective on the very nature of news and its espousal of journalistic values of impartiality and objectivity is one of the many tests it is facing. But for the moment, AJE's arrival should be celebrated for its attempt to correct the cultural and information bias of the main Western TV channels, while striving both to stick to balanced journalism and to put more emphasis on the understanding of developing countries. AJE should also be praised for bucking the general trend of presenting television news as 'infotainment', and for travelling in the opposite direction to most mainstream news organisations which are busy cutting their foreign news operations. If the channel survives with a healthy audience, then more news certainly will be good news.

Bibliography

Barkho, Leon, 'Unpacking the Discursive and Social Links in BBC, CNN and Al-Jazeera's Middle East Reporting', *Journal of Arab and Muslim Media Research*, 1/1 (Dec. 2007): pp. 11–30.

Boyd-Barrell, Oliver, 'Media Imperialism Reformulated', in D. K. Thussu (ed.), *Electronic Empires: Global Media and Local Resistance*, London: Arnold, 1998.

Chalaby, Jean, 'Transnational Television in Europe: The Role of Pan-European Channels', *European Journal of Communication*, 17/2 (2002): pp. 183–203.

Cunningham, Brent, 'Dave Marash: Why I Quit', *Columbia Journalism Review* (4 April 2008).

Curran, James, and Myung-Jin Park (eds), *De-Westernising Media Studies*, New York: Routledge, 2000.

Fox, Elizabeth, and Silvio Waisbord (eds), *Latin Politics, Global Media*, Austin, Tex.: University of Texas Press, 2002.

Kozloff, Nikolas, Hugo Chávez: *Oil, Politics, and the Challenge to the U.S.*, New York: Palgrave Macmillan, 2006.

Lawson, Chappell, and Sallie Hughes, 'Latin America's Postauthoritarian Media', in Milton, Andrew, and Rachel May (eds), *Uncivil Societies: Human Rights and Democratic Transitions in Eastern Europe and Latin America*, Lanham, Md.: Lexington, 2005.

Lugo-Ocando, Jairo (ed.), *The Media in Latin America*, Buckingham: Open University Press, 2008.

Lynch, Marc, *Voices of the New Arab Public*, New York: Columbia University Press, 2006.

Miles, Hugh, Al-Jazeera: *How Arab TV News Challenged the World*, London: Abacus, 2005.

Natarajan, K., and H. Xiaoming, 'An Asian Voice? A Comparative Study of Channel News Asia and CNN', *Journal of Communication*, 53/2 (2003): pp. 300–14.

Painter, James, 'The Boom in Counter-Hegemonic News Channels: A Case Study of Telesur', research paper presented to the Reuters Institute for the Study of Journalism, Oxford University, Feb. 2007, available at <http://reutersinstitute.politics.ox.ac.uk/fileadmin/documents/James_Painter.pdf>.

All Doom and Gloom? International TV Coverage of the April and May 2007 IPCC reports', paper presented at the Environmental Change Institute's Conference, 'Carbonundrums: Making Sense of Climate Change Reporting around the World', Oxford, 27 June 2007.

Pintak, Lawrence, 'Will Al-Jazeera English Find its Groove?', *Columbia Journalism Review* (30 Nov. 2006).

Rai, Mugdha, and Cottle, Simon 'Global Mediations: On the Changing Ecology of Satellite Television News', *Global Media and Communication* (April 2007).

Robertson, Alexa, 'Reporting the World Back to Itself', paper presented at SOAS conference, 'International Broadcasting, Public Diplomacy and Cultural Exchange', London, 17 Dec. 2007.

Sakr, Naomi, 'Al-Jazeera: Challenger or Lackey?', in Daya Thussu (ed.), *Media on the Move: Global Flow and Contra-Flow*, London and New York: Routledge, 2007.

Sinclair, John, *Latin American Television: A Global View*, Oxford: OUP, 1999.

'The Globalization of Latin Media', NACLA 37/4 (Jan.–Feb. 2004): pp. 15–19.

Thussu, Daya (ed.), *Electronic Empires: Global Media and Local Resistance*, London: Arnold, 1998.

(ed.), *Media on the Move: Global Flow and Contra-Flow*, London and New York: Routledge, 2007.

News as Entertainment: The Rise of Global Infotainment, London: Sage, 2007.

Zayani, Mohamed (ed.), *The Al-Jazeera Phenomenon: Critical Perspectives on New Arab Media*, London: Pluto, 2005.

Zhang, Xiaoling, 'CCTV International and Public Diplomacy', paper presented at SOAS conference, 'International Broadcasting, Public Diplomacy and Cultural Exchange', London, 19 Dec. 2007.

Acknowledgements

I am very grateful to several people who have helped with comments and encouragement on this study. I would particularly like to thank current and former staff of the Reuters Institute for the Study of Journalism (Paddy Coulter, John Lloyd and Sarmila Bose) for their support. Several colleagues from BBC Monitoring went way beyond the call of duty to provide me with information and recordings of the programmes monitored. My family gracefully put up with my obsession with the subject.

For the chapters on the boom in 24/7s and Telesur, the following offered invaluable advice: my supervisor Professor Daya Thussu; Dr Michelle Jackson who helped with the content analysis; Phil Gunson, Carlos Villalobos, Greg Morsbach, Carlos Chirinos, Adrian Fernandez, Olexiy Solohubenko, Ketan Chaukar and Hosam El Sokkari who put me right on several issues; Vin Ray, Lucio Mesquita and Nigel Chapman from the BBC who gave me the opportunity to study for one term as the BBC Fellow at the Reuters Institute. The views expressed in the study are of course not those of the BBC.

For the other chapters, Professor Larry Pintak, Nina Bigalke, Xiaoling Zhang and several current and former members of staff of Al Jazeera and the BBC Global News Division all offered good advice.

All errors of fact or judgement are of course my own.